Aiming at Amazon
The NEW Business of Self Publishing

— Aaron Shepard —

There has never been a self publishing manual like this.

Aiming at Amazon is *not* about getting your book into bookstores. Instead, it lays out an innovative approach that targets sales on Amazon.com. It reveals how to make a book sell well online, with tips never before offered. And it doesn't stop there—it gives you a way to publish your book that can double your profit per copy.

Avoid publishing plans that handicap you almost before you begin. Let *Aiming at Amazon* introduce you to the *new* business of self publishing.

"Aaron Shepard has been more successful selling through Amazon than any other self publisher I know, and this is the most comprehensive guide in print or online to marketing your book on the Amazon platform."

Morris Rosenthal, author,
Print-on-Demand Book Publishing

"Solid gold advice. . . . This book will give you the benefit of years of hard-earned experience."

Steve Weber, author, *Plug Your Book!*

"If you want to learn how to sell more books on Amazon, this is the best book I've read on the subject."

Stacie Vander Pol, author, *Top Self Publishing Firms*

"Shepard is considered one of the pioneers of marketing print-on-demand books through Amazon. . . . The model pioneered by Shepard, Rosenthal, and others is probably the best way for a newcomer to enter the world of self-publishing."

Peter Hupalo, *Midwest Book Review*

"Absolutely brimful of technical, hands-on advice."

Michael Allen, Grumpy Old Bookman (blog)

"An essential read for anyone having to market a self-published or POD-published book—and has a wealth of information for small press publishers, novice freelance book publicists, and mid-list authors of the larger publishing houses."

Jim Cox, *Jim Cox Reports*

"A truly great book that all of us should own (and actually read!). . . . If your efforts are focused on Amazon, this is the book."

Thomas Nixon, Degree Press and Small Press Blog

"A must-have book: pertinent, unduplicated, current, authoritative, and well-written. Has a maximum of useful information and a minimum of fluff, all written in an easy, understandable style. . . . Best advice available."

John Culleton, Wexford Press

"Revolutionary . . . . A must read for anybody who is considering self publishing without [wanting] too much hassle or expense."

Mayra Calvani, TCM Reviews

"Worthy of the confident air with which it's written. Whether you're small press or self-published, if you utilize POD and want to amp up your Amazon sales, you need this book! ... Even if you want to work within more traditional methods of bookselling, there's still plenty of valuable material here."

Lupa, Immanion Press

"A well-thought-out and well-researched system that provides a viable alternative .... With low up-front costs, and simple procedures that don't require specialized software, it's a method almost anyone can use."

Sheila Ruth, Imaginator Press

"Packed with practical techniques for today's savvy small publisher."

Susan Daffron, Logical Expressions, Inc.

"I sometimes wake up cold in the middle of the night, wondering where on earth I would be, career-wise, had *Aiming at Amazon* not been written. ... By an author, for authors, in a style that even head-in-the-cloud dreamers with ink in their veins can understand and act upon."

Barry Tighe, Can Write Will Write

"An amazing book and one of the most practical I've read. ... If you've self-published a book or are thinking about self-publishing, *Aiming at Amazon* is a must-read."

Tim Bete, director, Erma Bombeck Writers' Workshop, University of Dayton

"The perfect guide for the first-time publisher, [with] just enough information to inform but not overwhelm. . . . You won't find 'fad tricks' in this book, just solid advice."

Cheryl Kirk, Expanding Books

"Without *Aiming at Amazon,* I simply would not be where I am now. This month, I made what I would have made in six to eight months with the company I used previously for self publishing."

William Linney, Armfield Academic Press

"Absorbing. . . . Aaron Shepard is a savvy marketer. . . . Shepard writes simply but skips the chirpiness that mars many self-help books."

Marie Shear, *The Freelancer* (Editorial Freelancers Association newsletter)

"I've published ten other books through regular publishers, and this route is much more fun and rewarding!"

Ellen Hodgson Brown, Third Millennium Press

"Dramatically changed my direction in terms of publishing, and has turned a money-losing hobby into a growing, profitable business doing what I love the most."

Charles Sheehan-Miles, Cincinnatus Press

"Here's what [it] did for me: It gave me a business plan that was feasible, simple, low-cost and potentially VERY lucrative."

Darcy Pattison, Mims House

"What Aaron has done is to identify, analyze, and tweak the key factors that contribute to profitable sales at Amazon.com. . . . It's a great value for all authors."

Roger C. Parker, author, *Looking Good in Print*, and Webmaster, Published and Profitable

"Life-changing! . . . I purchased this book in early December. By late December I had founded my own company. I yanked one of my books away from a vanity press, re-edited, revised and republished the title. . . . In its first eight weeks, I made many times more money off this one book than I had in three years of working with POD publishers."

Nola Kelsey, Dog's Eye View Press

"Using the number-of-dog-eared-pages scale, this book should rank much higher than five stars."

James R. Holland, A Bit of Boston Books

"More than just a book. It's an entire system for setting up and running a profitable small book publishing company with no inventory, worldwide distribution, and as little as $100 up front."

David R. Yale, A Healthy Relationship Press

"A must read for any progressive self-publishing author."

Dehanna Bailee, author, *The ABC's of POD*

"The New Testament for the novice publisher. . . . Aaron Shepard shows how to exploit the new paradigm to the full."

Hedley Finger, Hand Holding Press

Also by Aaron Shepard

POD for Profit
More on the NEW Business of Self Publishing
(Forthcoming)

Perfect Pages
Self Publishing with Microsoft Word

The Business of Writing for Children
An Award-Winning Author's Tips on
Writing Children's Books and Publishing Them

Aiming at Amazon

The NEW Business of Self Publishing

OR

How to Publish Your Books with
Print on Demand and Online Book
Marketing on Amazon.com

Aaron Shepard

Shepard Publications
Friday Harbor, Washington

Author Online!

For updates and more resources,
visit Aaron Shepard's Publishing Page at

www. newselfpublishing.com

Author portrait by Wendy Edelson, www.wendyedelson.com

ISBN 978-0-938497-43-1

Library of Congress Control Number: 2006907458
Library of Congress subject headings:
Self-publishing
Books—Marketing
Amazon.com (Firm)
On-demand printing

Note: Aaron regrets he cannot provide private guidance in self
publishing. For additional resources, please see the appendix.

Version 2.1

The mind sees this forest better than the eye. The mind is not deceived by what merely shows.

H. M. Tomlinson
The Sea and the Jungle, 1912

When the bird and the book disagree, believe the bird.

John James Audubon

Chase two rabbits and catch none.

Russian proverb

Contents

About This Book   9

1   Aiming at Amazon   13

   Forget Bookstores   14
   Print on Demand   17
   Plan Your Route   21
   Go to the Source   24
   Ignore Amazon   30

2   Optimizing for Amazon   31

   Embrace the Possible   32
   Research the Market   35
   Optimize Your Title   39
   Write a Great Book   45
   Produce Your Pages   48
   Craft Your Cover   53
   Stick to a Format   57
   Collect Comments   58

3   Accessing Amazon   63

   Set Up Accounts   64
   Find Resources   66
   Make Contact   67
   Look Up Your Profile   70
   Keep Up with Change   71
   Take the Express   72

4 Marketing on Amazon   73

Check Your Listing   74
Claim Your Book   79
Make Corrections   82
Add Your Content   87
Submit a Cover Image   93
Share Other Images   98
Consider Inside Search   100
Suggest Tags   104
Categorize Your Book   109
Get Customer Reviews   111
Set Up Your Page   116
Explore More Options   121

5 Monitoring Amazon   131

Watch Availability   132
Watch Sales Ranks   135
Watch Search Results   141
Watch Pairings   143
Watch Rivalries   148
Watch Customer Reviews   153
Watch Tags   157
Watch Other Content   159

6 Pointing to Amazon   161

Channel Your Sales   162
Earn Commissions   164
Tame Your Links   166

7 Updating for Amazon   173

Refine Your Book   174
Refresh Your Content   176

8 Globalizing with Amazon   181

Aim at Amazons   182
Optimize for Amazons   183
Access Amazons   184
Market on Amazons   189
Monitor Amazons   198
Point to Amazons   199

Appendix   201

Where to Get Help   202
Amazon Etiquette   203
Kindle Books   204
Publishing Reprints   206
Removing a Listing   208
Rogue Sellers   209
Amazon Vendors   210
Amazon Ref Codes   211
The Book Depository   213
Replica Books   214
Self Publishing Terms   215

Index   217

About This Book

In recent years, self publishing has become big business. But not often for self publishers.

Though self publishing has been around for as long as there have been authors and the printers they could pay to work with them, it got a big boost in the mid-1980s. That was when personal computers, desktop laser printers, and desktop publishing software first allowed authors to compose their own print-ready pages.

But it was only in the late 1990s that self publishing really took off. In that period, the desktop publishing revolution was joined by the dual revolutions of print on demand and online bookselling. Together, these sparked a whole new industry of "self publishing companies"—an industry that has now made self publishing accessible to almost anyone who can type.

What has been largely lacking, though, is the know-how for making such publishing profitable. Though the classics on the business of self publishing—books by Dan Poynter, Tom and Marilyn Ross, and John Kremer—have all been revised in the decades since their first publications, they're still products of their time, focusing on the hard-to-crack world of bricks-and-mortar bookselling. They have little to say to those ready to exploit today's much more accessible opportunities online.

What we've needed, then, is a *new* business of self publishing.

That's exactly what I and a number of other self publishers have been working out over the past number of years. Many of us are earning a respectable profit from our work. Some, like myself, even make a reasonable living. Now I'd like to offer you the same possibilities.

This book will introduce that modern approach to self publishing for profit and then focus on marketing on Amazon, the best and biggest market for self publishers today. An upcoming book will discuss the print on demand service that offers by far the greatest profitability, and a projected third book may give tips on do-it-yourself book design.

I should mention up front that the *new* business of self publishing—just like old-style self publishing—is best suited to nonfiction. That's what is most likely to produce financial rewards, so it's the main concern of this book. But most of what's here will be useful for fiction publishing as well, and I do provide special tips for that.

Also, this book talks most about self publishing and marketing in the U.S., but it will be useful to self publishers in other countries as well. As long as you're publishing in English, the U.S. is likely your biggest potential market, and I'll tell you how to break into it from anywhere in the world. I also have a special chapter about selling internationally, for self publishers both inside and outside the U.S.

So, what can you reasonably hope for if you follow the path I lay out? Based on my experience, a nonfiction book that's well conceived and executed might sell between 50 and 200 copies a month—and continue to sell that many for years on end, with little ongoing effort—for a monthly profit of several hundred dollars. With luck, persistence, and a bit of brilliance, you might do a good deal better than that, as I've done now with several of my books.

This is all assuming, of course, that you handle the whole process competently—all the way from market research, through writing, design, production, and on to marketing.

That's a big "if"—but definitely within the reach of ordinary mortals.

A quick warning: By the time you read this book, it will be out of date. In fact, it will be out of date before it reaches the printer. Both Amazon and the field of print on demand are young and in constant flux. Writing about a moving target, I'm bound to include info already past its expiration date.

So, consider this book a starting point. Visit my Publishing Page to find any updates I've posted, especially in my Publishing Blog. While you're there, sign up for my email bulletin to receive notice of additional updates. Find me at

www. newselfpublishing.com

For alerts on new developments, as well as for general help, stay in dialog with other self publishers through email discussion lists and online forums. (See the appendix for suggestions.)

Above all, rely on yourself. Test everything here to see if it's still true. Discover what's changed.

Very little of the knowledge in this book came from inside sources. Most of it came from simple observation, reflection, and testing over many years by myself and fellow publishers. Now it's your turn. See what you can find, and share it with others. Keep exploring, keep experimenting.

I look forward to learning from you.

1
Aiming at Amazon

Forget Bookstores

Yes, I said it: *Forget bookstores.*

The first principle of the *new* business of self publishing is probably the hardest for aspiring publishers to accept. If you're like me, you love to visit your local bookstore—whether chain or independent—and wander the aisles, delighting in the sheer presence of so many enticing volumes. That love probably sprang up in your childhood, and will likely last you the rest of your life.

The trouble is, the feeling is not mutual.

In general, bookstores do not love self publishers. It's nothing personal. If the staff at that store all sat down and read your book, they might like it very much. They might even make an effort to promote it. Perhaps you can convince two or three local stores to do just that.

But for most bookstores, your book simply isn't worth the effort. The book business is a well-oiled machine that runs in broad and well-worn channels. Bookstores deal with sales reps and suppliers that can deliver dozens of titles at a time to their doorstep. Unless you already have a runaway bestseller, it's simply not efficient for them to deal with someone hawking one or two books. And to tell the truth, it's usually not worth *your* time to try to get them to.

Luckily, you no longer need to. With only minor effort and cost, you can get your book carried by the single bookseller that sells more books than the largest bookstore chain, handling nearly 20% of trade retail bookselling in the U.S.—about half of what's handled by all "real world" U.S. bookstores put together.* You can get your book on Amazon.com.

------

* Based on 2007 figures from R. R. Bowker's PubTrack Consumer.

Even better, on Amazon you'll compete on a much more level playing field with publishers of any size. By aiming at Amazon and exploiting its capabilities to the full, you can outmaneuver large publishers that may know less about its workings than you do and that have their main attention elsewhere.

Take the example of one of my own lead sellers, *The Business of Writing for Children.* For much of its publishing life, this book has been the biggest selling children's writing guide on Amazon.com. When *Aiming at Amazon,* the book you're reading, was first published, my children's writing book was competing on Amazon primarily against one guide from the For Dummies series and another from the Complete Idiot's series—*and it was outselling each of them by 2 to 1.*

Was it a better book than those others? I wouldn't make that claim. But by a combination of persistence, dedication, savvy, ingenuity, and skill, I was able to outmaneuver all comers and stay on top in Amazon sales.

In fact, by aiming at Amazon, I was able to sell close to 30% the number of copies sold by one of those nationally-distributed competitors *including its bookstore sales.* And because the profit from my publishing system is so high—generally half or more of the cover price—I was earning about twice as much in total as that author would make with a normal royalty.*

Once you accept the premise "Forget bookstores," it's amazing how much murkiness is instantly cleared out of the business of self publishing. Consider these:

• You don't have to design or commission a slick cover that will look at home on a bookstore shelf.

• You don't have to persuade anyone to stock your book.

---

* How do I know all this? The author is a friend of mine!

• You don't have to allow "returns"—copies sent back for refund when the bookseller won't wait longer to sell them.

• And best of all, you don't have to sit alone behind a stack of books at a tiny table in a busy bookstore and try to look like you want to be there.

Now, this doesn't mean that your book will never be sold in a bookstore. In most cases, it will. When you aim at Amazon, some customers will request your book from local bookstores—and most new channels for self publishing will make it easy for bookstores to get it. The difference is, if you follow the approach I most favor, those bookstores will obtain the book on *your* terms, not theirs.

Sound good? Keep reading, and I'll show you how to do it.

Print on Demand

Since you're already interested in self publishing, you've likely at least heard of author services like AuthorHouse, iUniverse, Xlibris, Trafford, Infinity Publishing, Lulu.com, Wordclay, Booklocker, Outskirts Press, and Amazon's own BookSurge and CreateSpace—services commonly called self publishing companies. You may also know that these businesses are based on *print on demand*—POD, for short.* Though this term describes a printing technology, it usually refers also to a distribution model—which, to the self publisher aiming at Amazon, is just as important.

From the technology standpoint, print on demand means printing books on computerized presses that use either lasers and toner or else liquid ink—in other words, on giant versions of a desktop laser or inkjet printer. Printing directly from computer files, these "digital presses" are able to efficiently produce even a single copy of a book at a time. This means a publisher no longer needs to invest in 1,000 or 2,000 or 5,000 copies of a book to bring the cost per copy down to a reasonable level. Now you can order only as many copies as you need, or none at all.

In fact, if you design your own book and produce the files, you can now set up a new title for just one to two hundred dollars—or in some cases, even for free. Cost is no longer a huge factor in deciding to publish, because your only significant printing expense comes as you're selling books!

Are there any drawbacks? Of course. In exchange for the lower entry cost, you get a higher cost per copy. And regardless of what you might hear, print-on-demand books don't yet quite

---

* It's pronounced not as an acronym but as initials—"PEE-o-DEE." We're not pod people!

match the quality of most books produced by traditional, offset printing (also called litho printing, or offset litho). Still, most people truly can't see the difference, and both quality and cost are good enough that even major publishers now use POD both to keep slower-selling titles in print and to meet urgent demand for new ones.

That's the hardware angle. To understand print on demand as a distribution model, you need to know a little about how the industry is set up.

Most people assume that the big self publishing companies print the books they sell, but mostly they don't. In the U.S. and Canada, such companies rely partly or entirely on two major POD providers. The relatively new kid on the block is Amazon's own POD business, which U.S. companies access through the Publisher Services division of Amazon's subsidiary, BookSurge. By using Amazon POD, self publishing companies can get direct distribution into Amazon in the U.S. as well as into Amazon in the U.K. and Germany—with more Amazon sites sure to follow.*

The older, more established, and much larger POD provider is Lightning Source Inc. Don't know much about it? Or anything about it at all? I wouldn't be surprised. Lightning—as I'll often call it for short—may not even want you to!

Just like BookSurge Publisher Services, Lightning Source chooses to deal with publishers and self publishing companies rather than with authors directly. But while BookSurge will try to steer authors to its author services division, Lightning doesn't want that business at all. Instead, it happily lets the great majority of self publishing companies act as "front ends" for the operation—taking your book, producing the files needed

---

* Reportedly, even Amazon POD doesn't print all its own books. As of 2009, some of its printing is said to be farmed out to a company called ePAC.

for print on demand, and handling all the submission and administrative details.

But let's get back to distribution. Lightning's importance to the POD industry is largely due to a unique advantage: It's part of the same company that houses Ingram Book Company, the biggest book wholesaler in the U.S.* Almost all bookstores in the country, as well as many libraries and schools, order books from Ingram.

As you might expect, Lightning has a direct line into Ingram. In fact, Ingram offers every title printed by Lightning, listing it as immediately available. Lightning also fills orders directly from some of the largest U.S. booksellers, including Barnes & Noble and Baker & Taylor, the second largest U.S. wholesaler and a primary supplier of Borders. So, by working with *any* of the self publishing companies that use Lightning Source, you can automatically make your book available to booksellers throughout the U.S.

Foremost among these booksellers is Amazon.com. If Amazon POD isn't already printing your book, Amazon will still automatically list it from data sent by Lightning and Ingram and will then order from one or the other of those two as need arises. And because Amazon regularly uses Ingram for drop shipping, all Lightning books are listed on Amazon as in stock and available within 24 hours, whether or not Amazon has its own copies.

Another, ever-growing benefit provided by Lightning Source is an international reach. Lightning already has one major branch in the U.K., with another branch projected for Australia or Southeast Asia. At the same time, Lightning's wholesale customers in both the U.S. and the U.K. themselves

---

* In this book, I'll use "Ingram" to refer to Ingram Book Company rather than to either of the Ingram-branded entities encompassing both that wholesaler and Lightning Source.

sell internationally. The upshot is that every Lightning book is available from online booksellers throughout much of the world. (That includes five Amazon sites outside the U.S., which is more than is yet done by Amazon POD!)

So, just as print on demand can remove cost as a deciding factor in publishing, it can also remove what has traditionally been the biggest roadblock for self publishers: lack of access to the channels of distribution. What's more, it does this in a way that eliminates most of the ongoing labor of publishing. Success no longer means you must spend your time taking orders, shipping copies, and sending invoices and reminders for payment.

Instead, just let booksellers, schools, and libraries order your book from one of their usual suppliers. Then all you need do is sit back and wait for your monthly check. In fact, except for maybe keeping a few copies for promotion and gifts, you don't need to stock your book at all. (And as one who remembers having a hallway full of book cartons in the "old days," I can't begin to tell you what a blessing that is.)

So, you should run right out and sign up with one of the self publishing companies, right?

Maybe not!

Plan Your Route

If you're aiming at Amazon, the diverse field of print on demand offers a variety of routes to your goal. One may be better suited to publishing newcomers with little technical knowledge or skill. One may appeal to the more confident or budget-conscious. And for the most ambitious and capable, one may provide the way to highest profit.

Let's start with what I call "full-service" self publishing companies. I've already mentioned some of the most popular ones: AuthorHouse, iUniverse, Xlibris, Trafford, Infinity Publishing, Wordclay, Booklocker, Outskirts Press, and the self publishing division of Amazon's own BookSurge. These "author services" will take your manuscript, transform it into a book, and arrange for printing and distribution through Lightning Source, Amazon POD, or both.

If you have no clue how to publish a book and just want someone to take care of most of it for you, then a full-service company is probably your best bet. The main drawback is that you pay heavily for that assistance, and not just in setup fees. The percentage that these companies take for being middlemen with the big POD providers is no doubt well earned, but it about doubles the book's cost to you per copy. That shows up either as a reduced "royalty" for you, or as a minimum cover price high enough to make the book less competitive.

Still, what you lose in money, you gain in time. A full-service company lets you publish simply and get on with your life. For help in choosing such a company, you might look at *The Fine Print of Self Publishing,* by Mark Levine, and *Top Self Publishing Companies,* by Stacie Vander Pol.

Another kind of self publishing company is what I call "self-service." This kind of company aims at self publishers who will take more responsibility for their own books—or else be less concerned about professional standards. All business is conducted online. Personal assistance is minimal, except what can be found in help pages, customer forums, and the like.

The first of these companies was Lulu.com, and it's still at least one of the biggest and most popular. With its low-cost setup for printing with full distribution, Lulu finally made publishing accessible to almost anyone. It's a brilliant model, really, and we have a lot to thank Lulu for. But Lulu is still a middleman, and its customers still pay for that with a high cost per copy.

One self-service company, though, is different: the book division of CreateSpace. Launched as Amazon's answer to Lulu, it joined BookSurge as a sister gateway to Amazon POD.

While CreateSpace's book business in most ways follows Lulu's model, it's also what you might call a factory outlet. Since its parent company owns the presses, CreateSpace can and does radically undercut the per-copy costs of other self publishing companies. The upshot is, with CreateSpace, you can get much closer to a decent profit margin. *Much* closer.

But there are drawbacks here too. The biggest one is limited distribution. CreateSpace will not make your book directly available to any other online bookseller, any real-world bookstore, or any wholesaler. The book won't even be available to Amazon outside the U.S.—though that is likely to change before long. Still, your book will be on Amazon.com, and that's what matters most.

The other drawback is that CreateSpace does not yet have a set of tools for automated book file creation that can always match Lulu's. That's an especial problem when coupled with the lack of personal assistance. But this too is likely to change before long—and quite possibly by the time you read this.

Despite its current weaknesses, I believe CreateSpace offers most self publishers the best balance between convenience and profitability. More than any other "author service," CreateSpace is a fine choice for aiming at Amazon.

You can find CreateSpace at

www.createspace.com

If you need guidance on dealing with it, you can find that in *The Step-By-Step Guide to Self-Publishing for Profit!*, by C. Pinheiro and Nick Russell.

CreateSpace may be a self publisher's best choice among author services, but that's not saying some of us can't do better. For highest profit, let's take a look beyond author services entirely.

Go to the Source

For the most profitable publishing with print on demand, the service you use must start by offering three things:
- A low setup cost.
- A low per-copy cost (compared to typical POD costs).
- Wide distribution.

As we've seen, most self publishing companies fail to meet at least two of these requirements, and none meets them all. For maximum profit, then, you need to forget *author* services and turn instead to a *publisher* service. And not to BookSurge Publisher Services, which skews its terms heavily toward Amazon and doesn't want to talk to you anyway if you've published fewer than fifty books. No, you need to work *directly* with the greatest POD provider of them all, Lightning Source Inc.

But wait. Lightning works with publishers and self publishing companies, not authors. So, how can you deal with it directly?

Simple. You can become a publisher. And thankfully, Lightning Source makes that step easier than ever before.

Though there are a number of things you might need or want to do in setting up a publishing business, only two are vital for working with Lightning: adopting a publishing name and acquiring a set of ISBNs—International Standard Book Numbers.* You don't even have to be in the U.S. or the U.K., where Lightning's branches are, because it can handle publishers anywhere in the world.

---

* Don't confuse a book's ISBN with its *bar code*—the set of bars that appears on the book's back cover and *encodes* the ISBN. To work with Lightning, you must acquire ISBNs yourself but *not* the corresponding bar codes.

I'll caution you right now, though, that working with Lightning Source is not the best choice, or even a good one, for most self publishers. This route will suit you only if you're:

• Planning to publish more than one book. The setup and learning probably won't be worth it for just one or two.

• Profit-oriented. Willing to make the extra effort to earn a good return on your investment.

• A good marketer. You won't make money if you're not willing and able to promote your book, at least at the start.

• Financially able. It takes money to make money, and you'll have to be ready to plunk down cash when needed (though what's needed can be much, much less than with full-service self publishing companies or old-style self publishing).

• Possessing a good business attitude. That means being able to work with others in the industry professionally and courteously, without undue suspiciousness or an attitude of "us against them."

• Technically capable. Able to work with computers effectively and to understand complex instructions. To produce the files Lightning needs to print your book, you'll have to perform a variety of demanding tasks in complicated software with minimal help from Lightning itself. If you have no knowledge of desktop publishing, you'll have to learn it or be willing to engage others to do it for you.*

I can't stress this last point enough. If you're the kind of person who often gets stuck on the computer and needs to be bailed out by others, do yourself a favor and stay away from Lightning Source! Lightning is set up to work with professionals who don't need such help, and you simply won't get it.

Though the demands are great, so can be the rewards—quite simply, that you can double your profit per copy. Yes,

---

* To find consultants who can help you, see the "Other Resources" listings on my Publishing Page. And no, I don't offer such services myself!

that's how working directly with Lightning Source compares financially to working with most self publishing companies. That's because there's one more vital factor in profitable publishing with print on demand: control over discount.

Lightning is the only POD service that offers such control in so great a range. Standard discounts in the book industry run about 40% for bookstores, 55% for wholesalers, and 65% for distributors. But Lightning allows you to set a "short discount" of as little as 20%.

Let's see how this plays out in practice. We'll imagine you have a hundred-page book with a cover price of $10. Lightning Source receives an order for a copy from one of its bookselling partners—Ingram, Amazon, B&N, or another. After Lightning prints and ships the copy, it takes your cover price and deducts your 20% discount as well as its own printing charges. (Shipping charges are paid by the bookseller, so they're out of the equation.) The whole thing looks like this:

Cover price	$10.00
Discount (20%)	−$2.00
Gross profit	$8.00
Printing cost	−$2.30
Net profit	$5.70

One thing you may notice in this example is that there's no "royalty." That's because Lightning Source is a publisher service, not an author service! With Lightning, you don't make royalties, you make profits. That's what that bottom figure is, and that's exactly what Lightning sends to you.

Another thing you may notice is that the figure at the bottom—yes, that money you get from Lightning—is well over half the cover price of the book! Now, where else in the world of print on demand—or for that matter, in the worlds of old-style self publishing or conventional trade publishing—will you find a profit margin like that?

But can a short discount hurt your book? In a way, yes—because it means no bookstore will be willing to stock it. But as I said at the start, stocking in bookstores is highly unlikely for a self-published book anyway. So, why gamble half your profit on a bad bet?

More to the point, our main target, Amazon.com, shows no reluctance to ordering or even stocking books with short discounts. In fact, at this writing, Amazon is selling many such books to its customers at 10% off the cover price! Among the independent self publishers I know who are working with Lightning today, most offer a short discount of 20% and have no trouble from it.

But at this point, I know some of you are asking, *Is this book completely outdated? Now that Amazon does its own POD, hasn't it stopped buying all books from Lightning Source?*

That's what Amazon has many self publishers believing. But the real answer is a definite no.

Yes, it's true that Amazon.com has announced a policy of selling POD books only if printed by itself or bought through its program for small publishers, Amazon Advantage—a program that demands the outrageous discount of 55%. And it's also true that Amazon has now strong-armed most large Lightning clients to sign up with BookSurge's Publisher Services division as well. But what's also true and less well know is that Amazon's campaign has completely ignored smaller businesses. In fact, the smallest company Amazon seems to have bothered with has published about 150 books!

To my knowledge at this writing, *not a single independent self publisher has been affected in any way by Amazon's "policy."* So for now, and for the foreseeable future, you can feel

confident about working with Lightning alone. It's highly unlikely that Amazon will ever care enough to trouble you.

And if I'm wrong? If Amazon does someday decide to shut
out *all* Lightning books?

Assuming Amazon could even pull that off—which for
technical reasons, I doubt—self publishers working with Lightning would still be ahead of the game. All POD contracts are
nonexclusive, meaning you could sign up with Amazon POD
while still working with Lightning—just as the self publishing
companies and other large Lightning clients have done.

In that case, Amazon POD would print copies for Amazon,
while Lightning would print them for everyone else—other
online booksellers, bookstores with requests from customers,
and so on. If you like, Lightning could even keep printing
copies sold on Amazon outside the U.S. Though Amazon POD
is now available in the U.K., Amazon has declared it will *not*
discriminate there against books from other providers.

In fact, working with Lightning would still even help with
copies sold on Amazon right in the U.S. Despite its aggressive
moves, Amazon POD doesn't yet have the capacity to print all
the copies it needs of all the books it's grabbing. When it falls
behind, where do you think it picks up extra copies? Ingram, of
course, with its copies printed by Lightning, providing a higher
profit margin to Lightning's clients.

What's more, Amazon knows which books are available
through wholesalers and which aren't. If you work with Amazon POD alone, Amazon knows that customers can't buy the
book elsewhere—so it gets sold at full price. But if it's also a
Lightning book listed by Ingram, Amazon will likely discount
it—which should increase your sales.

I'll have much, much more to say about working with
Lightning Source in my upcoming book *POD for Profit*. For
now, you can find both the U.S. and U.K. branches at

www.lightningsource.com

For ISBNs, contact the official agency that handles registrations for your country—not a third party! To find that agency, you can search online for your country and "ISBN." For the U.S., it's R. R. Bowker at

www.isbn.org

Be careful! Bowker will urge you to buy other products and services, but the *only* thing you need are the ISBNs.*

---

* Bowker also maintains a site at www.myidentifiers.com specially for self publishers—but it's mainly a way to charge you extra for services normally offered to publishers for free. Avoid this site!

Ignore Amazon

Self publishers using print on demand are sometimes confused about how to sell copies of their books to Amazon. So, let me make one thing crystal clear: **You do *not* sell your books to Amazon.**

With POD, Amazon does *not* buy copies from you. It buys them from your POD service or a wholesaler, but *never* from you directly. All Amazon sales are handled for you, without any involvement on your part.

Let's get even more specific. You do *not* have to sell copies through Amazon Advantage, Amazon's program for small publishers. And considering that Advantage demands a 55% discount, makes you pay shipping, and only pays when the copies are sold, that's about the last thing you'd want to do! In fact, one of the chief benefits of POD is exactly that it enables small publishers to get around Advantage.

Self publishers using POD may also wonder whether they should sell books directly to customers through Amazon Marketplace, Amazon's venue for third-party vendors.* I have nothing against Marketplace, but with print on demand, you really don't need it. You can earn about as much money per copy when going through normal POD channels—and without the hassle of filling orders and dealing with customers.

So, why bother? Take it easy. Just sit back and enjoy the ride.

---

* Such selling is covered in detail in Steve Weber's *Sell on Amazon: A Guide to Amazon's Marketplace, Seller Central, and Fulfillment by Amazon Programs.*

2
Optimizing for Amazon

Embrace the Possible

In an interview, Steve Jobs of Apple once explained his company's different attitude toward technology. Most companies, he said, decide what product they'd like to make, then try to force existing technology to serve it, whether that technology is ready or not. Apple, on the other hand, has ideas about what it wants to make, but waits and watches—sometimes for years—for the needed technology to develop. Then it designs its products around the technology.

Though I was fairly quick to recognize the potential in the conjunction of print on demand and online bookselling, I still had to figure out what kinds of projects it could best serve. These two phenomena, together and apart, have very particular strengths. And it was only by matching my projects to those strengths that I've managed to shape a successful publishing program.

Let me point out a few things that work well in the *new* business of self publishing. Keep in mind I'm *not* saying you *shouldn't* publish other kinds of books. I've often published other kinds myself, just for the love of it. But I know ahead of time when publishing a book is likely to bring in substantial money, and when it's mostly for my own pleasure. And you should know it too.

Nonfiction. One of Amazon's greatest contributions has been to make lesser-known books visible by providing a way to search for them. But this only helps if people are looking. The main beneficiary, then, has been nonfiction in established areas of interest. If you're aiming at Amazon with the idea of making money, nonfiction is your best bet.

Conversely, it's much harder to do well with fiction. Though Amazon has been gradually developing better tools for selling fiction, far fewer people are likely to ever know your book is there.

Medium-length books. Though initial investment is lower with print on demand, the cost per copy is higher than in traditional book printing, and most of the difference is in the cost per page. To keep the cover price reasonable, then, you'll probably want to keep your books of moderate length. Of the books I've published so far, nearly all are under 200 pages.

Luckily, this ties into what Amazon's customers want. At least for nonfiction, people *prefer* books that aren't too long. Most don't have time for long ones. I sometimes think the popularity of my book *The Business of Writing for Children*— just over a hundred pages—comes partly from its being so much shorter than its competitors. In fact, I suspect people will often pay *more* for brevity.

There are limits, though, on the short side too. Lightning Source, for instance, cannot make a black-and-white paperback shorter than forty-eight pages. (CreateSpace lets you go down to twenty-four.) And in any case, though many Amazon customers don't want their books *too* long, some may complain if a book is less than "full-length"—even if priced accordingly!

Simple layouts. The black-and-white POD presses now used by the big providers can print photos and other graphics that are not likely to disappoint you. But because these presses are high-speed, exact placement on the page is dicey. Though you're permitted to make your graphics "bleed"—extend past the page edge slightly to keep any white from showing there— white strips may still appear. So, if your black-and-white book depends on bleed, you're out of luck with POD.

Black and white, or limited color. The big POD providers now offer full-color printing as well as black and white—but at current prices, you would be hard-pressed to make a profit from it. This is especially true with POD by Lightning Source, where you must also deal with limited binding choices and quirky layout requirements. (At this writing, CreateSpace is a better choice for most full-color books.)

Beyond that, children's picture books—one of the main uses of such printing—almost never do well on Amazon, no matter who publishes them. Most such books are bought by parents and grandparents browsing in bookstores. So, if you're looking to make money on Amazon, a children's picture book is one of the last things to try.

Still, color POD is one example of how technologies available to small publishers continue to develop and make new kinds of books practical. Color printing has become a high priority in the POD world, and the next two or three years are expected to see the arrival of new inkjet presses that will increase speed, raise quality, and cut costs dramatically.

I plan to have my books ready for them!

Research the Market

Before committing yourself to months or even years of developing a book, you owe it to yourself to get an idea of the book's potential for sales. Of course, you don't have to limit yourself to publishing potential bestsellers, but you do want as accurate as possible an idea of what to expect.

My own way to get this is to go on Amazon.com and study the bestsellers in the field I want to write in. I especially take note of their sales ranks. For nonfiction, the top books' sales ranks reflect not just the quality and marketing of the books, but also the interest in that field among Amazon customers. Since you can only sell to people who are interested enough to find your book, the top sales ranks in your book's field suggest the most sales you can expect.

Sales ranks, though, don't actually measure sales. They only tell how much a book has sold recently on Amazon *in relation to other books*. The lower the number, the more the book has recently sold comparatively. For instance, the book with the sales rank of #1 has lately been selling more than the book that's #2. From observation, I can also tell you that every time the average sales rank doubles, the actual sales have been less by about half. In other words, a book averaging 10,000 has been selling about half as much as a book averaging 5,000.

Sales of used copies affect a book's sales rank right along with sales of new ones. The sales ranks of a book's different formats, though—paperback, hardcover, and so on—are figured separately.

Currently, sales ranks for *all* books are revised every hour, all at the same moment. (And yes, much of the info you read about this on the Web and even in newly-published books is out of date—usually by many years.)

Unfortunately, Amazon has now programmed this function to have a very short memory. So, it doesn't take many sales to boost a book's rank dramatically, and it doesn't take a long period of inaction for the rank to drop back down. As time goes on, these shifts seem to become more and more extreme. For this reason, you must keep an eye on a book over a period of time to get a true sense of where it stands.

But what exactly do those ranks mean in terms of sales? Well, it changes over time, and even from one season to another. But here are the general guidelines I use, regarding a book's typical range:

• Top 10,000. If you can get your book here and keep it here much of the time, you have a real winner. A book with an average rank of 5,000 might sell 250 copies a month.

• 10,000 to 50,000. A very good performer.

• 50,000 to 200,000. Not a hot item, but still a respectable earner.

• Over 200,000. Don't do it for the money.

For a more rigorous, up-to-date look, visit my publishing buddy Morris Rosenthal, who has been tracking and calculating sales ranks for years. You'll find his most recent results at

www.fonerbooks.com/surfing.htm

Because Amazon's sales ranks are now so fleeting, you may want to use one of the Web-based tools available for following them. One is my own free Sales Rank Express. Among other functions, it lets you look up a book and then its top ten "pairings"—titles used by Amazon for its "Also Bought" listings—with their sales ranks. This can give you a very quick overview of the most popular books in that field. You'll find this free service at

www.salesrankexpress.com

I'll have more to say on sales rank tools in my chapter on monitoring Amazon.

Once you've figured the top sales potential of books in a given field, you must still try to realistically assess your chances of competing in it. Because I'm a good, experienced writer and an expert marketer on Amazon, I figure I can usually match or at least come close to the sales ranks of the bestsellers I study. (So far, my record has been pretty good.)

But sometimes this requires deciding on the best approach. Will you try to compete head on by writing a book covering the same ground the bestsellers do, or will you write a book that complements them?

For instance, the leading book in the field of self publishing—both on Amazon and in bookstores—is Dan Poynter's *Self-Publishing Manual*. It has been the leading book for decades. Though Dan has shown no special expertise in Amazon marketing—and has no need of it either—his position from other efforts and from word of mouth is unassailable. So, any author going head to head with him by writing a general book on self publishing is committing publishing suicide.

But what if a book appeared on Amazon offering a fresh angle—a specialized approach that Dan's book almost completely ignores, that's innovative and up-to-date, that's more in tune with a new wave of self publishers, and that appeals in a special way to enthusiastic users of Amazon? Would those customers buy that book *along with* Dan's, if not by itself?

And what if that book complemented not only Dan's but also every other top self publishing book on Amazon? Could that book compete with Dan's in sales rank? Or even surpass it?

You'll find the answers in the sales ranks of the book now in your hands. (And if you want to influence that rank, you can write a customer review!)

Obviously, using Amazon to research markets is most helpful for nonfiction—and as I said before, nonfiction is what works best anyway in online bookselling. But these ideas can help with fiction too if you're willing to target your book to a specific interest group.

For instance, my wife, Anne L. Watson, is a budding author with two (self-published) novels already to her credit. Her first novel features a cat, her second one features puppets, and another still to come features carousels. Each of these subjects has an interest group attached, and you can compare their strengths on Amazon.

You can also measure interest in a novel's setting. Anne's second novel, for instance, takes place partly in New Orleans. Though that setting was chosen for other reasons, I'm sure Amazon would verify that New Orleans will sell more books than Des Moines!

Optimize Your Title

I once heard the outrageously popular children's author R. L. Stine say that he had to have a great title for a book before he would write it. And sometimes he would write a book just *because* he had a great title.

I'm not much different. For me, the title generally comes soon after the book idea—sometimes within minutes, or even seconds. If it doesn't, it's hard for me to think seriously about writing the book. A good title becomes a core around which the book is written. And when your book is finally published, your title needs just that kind of magnetism to draw people's attention and make them look closer.

That's true not just on Amazon, but anywhere. But on Amazon, it's not enough.

When you aim at Amazon, it helps to consider your title as two distinct components. Focusing your book and attracting customers is the job of the main title. The subtitle, on the other hand, has wholly different functions. First and foremost, it must make the book *findable*.

As I said, one of Amazon's greatest contributions has been to make lesser-known books visible by providing a way to search for them. This is, in fact, part of what makes the *new* business of self publishing viable. And it is your book's subtitle that provides your best opportunity to be picked up in search results.

If you've ever developed a Web site, you've probably heard of SEO—*search engine optimization*. This stands for planting keywords in your pages so, when people search for something on Google or another search engine, your site will show up prominently in results. On Amazon, you do nearly the same thing by planting keywords in your subtitle.

Take my book *The Business of Writing for Children*. The full subtitle of this book is—let me take a deep breath—*An Award-Winning Author's Tips on Writing Children's Books and Publishing Them, or How to Write, Publish, and Promote a Book for Kids.*

Unwieldy? Certainly—and not much of an ad for my writing skills, either! But take a close look at it, then try to think of what search phrase you would personally use to find such a book. You'll likely find, whatever you come up with, that all the words of that phrase are contained within that subtitle. Maybe not in the same order, but still there and ready to be found.

What does that mean on Amazon? When anyone searches for such a book, my book's competitors might each show up some or even most of the time. But *my* book will come up *almost every time.* So, I will have that many more opportunities to sell it.

Also, here's a fine point about that subtitle that you might not catch: It includes the *exact* phrase "writing children's books," which seems to be the one phrase most commonly used to look for this kind of book. I could have more elegantly said "writing and publishing children's books"—but the presence of the exact words in the exact order boosts a book in Amazon search results for that phrase. Positioning the phrase close to the beginning would have helped too, though this subtitle of mine scores no points for that.

The keywords you choose can not only help your book reach the market you wrote it for, it can also help it spread out to other ones. For instance, I've published a series of books on reader's theater, a simple form of dramatics often used in classrooms. It's not yet that big a market, so my books can only do so well in it.

At some point, though, I realized that these books of mine had appeal also as collections of "children's plays"—and that the market for that was bigger than the reader's theater market! By adding "children's plays" into my subtitles, I was able to sell successfully to a whole new set of customers, and in the process outsell all other books on reader's theater.

For a novel, you're not likely to want as comprehensive a subtitle as for a nonfiction book, but if you're targeting a specific interest group, you can definitely be helped by at least a brief one. For instance, my wife, Anne's, first novel, featuring a cat, is called *Skeeter: A Cat Tale.*

While a good main title is usually the result of quick inspiration, an optimized subtitle for a nonfiction book generally takes much elbow grease. Though I come up with most of my main titles almost immediately, a subtitle takes me hours, and I'm likely to return to it many times over the course of working on the book.

To find the right keywords, I've relied on the same tools I've used for optimizing my Web sites, including the venerable WordTracker, at

www.wordtracker.com

Today this service has many competitors, and you can find them by searching the Web for "keyword tool." Some have impressive new features, but you'll have to judge their effectiveness for yourself.*

A newer, free service is Google Insights for Search, with many interesting features. Find it at

www.google.com/insights/search

---

* One tool claims it can tell you the search phrases used by Amazon customers—but this is based on data from a sampling of computer users with a certain browser toolbar, not data from Amazon itself. For a niche market especially, the results could be misleading.

You can also get suggestions from any Google search results page. Near the top left, click on "Show Options," then on "Related Searches."

Amazon itself can provide hints on popular search terms. As you start typing your own terms into a search box, Amazon will suggest terms used by others that have the same beginning. Also, for the more common searches, Amazon will generally display at the top of search results a brief list of "Related Searches"—other terms used by customers with similar interests. If you see this list, you'll know that the search term you used was popular, plus you'll have Amazon's suggestions for additional terms.

Of course, I also study titles of other books in the field I'm targeting. One good way to find more on Amazon is to click from one book's "Also Bought" list to another. Or access the same data more efficiently with the "Get Pairings" buttons in Sales Rank Express results.

But how do you fit in all those keywords? One option is to create a "two-tiered" subtitle. You may have noticed I did this with the subtitle for *The Business of Writing for Children*. The first tier is *An Award-Winning Author's Tips on Writing Children's Books and Publishing Them*. The second one, connected by an *or,* is *How to Write, Publish, and Promote a Book for Kids*.

This structure lets me include two different forms of the words *write, publish,* and *book,* as well as both *children's* and *kids*. And yes, you do need to include word variants if you want them found. Amazon—unlike Google and some other search engines—will not automatically look for them.

Subtitles on Amazon have another function too. They must tell the customer as much as possible about what's inside the book. In search results, or in various listings of recommended books, you get no more than a cover image and a title to convince the customer to take a closer look. The more your title tells about what your book contains, the more likely the customer will find something of interest and click through.

Of course, fitting in lots of keywords *and* telling customers as much as you can about content can result in quite a long subtitle. But this in itself can be a plus. The longer your title, the more "shelf space" you get on Amazon's pages. The title length itself will draw attention.

In constructing a longer subtitle, you have a real advantage over other writers and publishers. Most of them would nearly die of embarrassment to display a long, inelegant subtitle on Amazon. It goes against everything they've been taught about good writing style. That's fine, because it means more business for you!

But just how long a subtitle are we talking about here? That depends in part on the length of your main title. Amazon will accept a total of 200 characters for main title and subtitle *combined*. (And yes, that's counting spaces and punctuation, including the colon and space between main title and subtitle.) If Amazon receives any more than that 200, it *truncates* the subtitle when displaying it online—and the characters aren't taken off the end but out of the middle, replaced by an ellipsis!

So, subtract the length of your main title from that 200 characters. That's what you have free for your subtitle (including the colon and space).

Now, say you have a main title of 25 characters and a subtitle of 150 characters. You're within Amazon's bounds, but there's one more problem: Not all listings outside Amazon will accept so much. For instance, Ingram will drop any characters in your subtitle past the first 116, while Baker & Taylor will allow it only 113. (Note that this time we're talking about the length of the subtitle *alone,* since Lightning, Ingram, and

B&T—unlike Amazon—all handle subtitles *separately* from main titles.)

The solution? Create two versions of the subtitle: a "full" version, then a "short" one with a maximum of 100 characters for anywhere the full one won't fit. You might also create a third and even shorter subtitle for wherever you need one that *does* sound elegant. Then you'll be ready for anything! (I'll tell you later how to get the "full" version of your subtitle onto Amazon.)

In Amazon's early days, your book's title was the *only* means to get the book shown in search results. That's no longer true. Amazon's default search order, which it calls "Relevance," looks also at buying patterns, Search Inside text, the book's product description, and more. So, a book might place high in search results even if the title doesn't use the search phrase.

Still, optimizing your title is the simplest, most direct, and most immediate way to get Amazon to show your book when people are looking. So, you want to make sure you include at least all the most important key words and phrases.

One final caution: This isn't a license to throw your words together just any which way! Yes, include your keywords, but make sure your subtitle is—if not elegant—at least coherent, focused, and cleanly structured, regardless of length. It won't do any good to display your book's title to customers if it only turns them off!

Write a Great Book

This is a step that many self publishers neglect.*

Self publishing companies often lure prospects by talking about all the worthwhile manuscripts the big publishing houses pass over. There's some truth in this, but it masks a bigger truth: The great majority of submissions are unpublishable— some say as many as 90%.

Even if you're publishing yourself, don't let your writing fall in that 90%. It's true that a mediocre book can do well on Amazon for a while, just on the strength of its marketing. But sooner or later the customer reviews catch up with you, as disappointed readers do their best to save others from the experience. It doesn't take many such reviews to stop others from giving your book a try. But even if you could get away with it, wouldn't you rather write a book you can be proud of?

If you don't have much writing experience, take time to start learning the craft. (And I do mean "start," because it's a lifelong process!) Read some books about the kind of writing you want to do, or take a class. Read and *analyze* examples of great writing. Read Strunk and White's *The Elements of Style.*

Write, rewrite, polish. Rare is the author who can make everything work on the first try. And don't just cut and paste heedlessly. Check what comes before and after your edits, to make sure you've maintained flow and consistency.

If your book needs photos or illustrations, start planning for that early. Make sure you get high-quality originals, and also make sure you have any permission you need to use them. Don't just pull photos, art, or other graphics from the Web.

---

* OK, if you're already a successful published writer, you can skip this section. It won't say much you don't know.

Such images are seldom of high enough quality to appear in print, and they may be protected by copyright.

Feedback is essential in writing almost any book. There are always problems or omissions that you can't see because you're too close to the writing or to the subject. For nonfiction, I commonly seek comments both from experts on my book's subject, and from beginners who can tell me where I've assumed too much knowledge in the reader. For fiction, I've found that belonging to a critique group with other writers in my genre is invaluable.

There are few people, though, who are both qualified and willing to help you improve your writing by putting it under a magnifying glass. That's why almost any writer needs an editor. If you aim to produce high-quality work, figure on hiring an editor as an essential part of the writing process.

In fact, if you can afford the money and the time, hire two. Get a *general editor* to edit your content, and a *copyeditor* to check all the nitpicky little details of spelling, grammar, and consistency of language and punctuation. The big publishers all give their books to each kind of editor—and this makes a lot of sense, since the two jobs require completely different mind-sets and collections of skills.

Now, when I tell you to hire one or more editors, this is strictly a case of "Do as I say, not as I do." I did hire an editor for my first commercial self-published book, decades ago. Since then, though, I've developed a reputation for clean prose among editors who have bought my work, so I feel confident about editing myself. Still, I do it with the knowledge that there are bound to be errors that slip past, and with the prayer that none will be serious.

One of the most important writing tips I can give you is to take breaks from your writing, especially at the point when you think you're "done." I'm not talking about a day or two—more like a couple of months or more. Use the time to get feedback from friends, or to read books on writing, or to work on your Web site, or to learn your desktop publishing software. Chances are, you'll come back to your book knowing exactly what it needs to make it twice as good.

Produce Your Pages

A book is not an office document or a Web site. Books have their own visual language. It's not that hard to learn that language, but figure it in as part of your learning process if you're going to design your own pages instead of hiring a professional. An amateurish look to your book will make your content suspect—and you don't want Amazon's customer reviewers complaining about it either.

At the same time, your pages do not have to look like they're from a slick magazine. In fact, you don't want them to. A book is not a magazine either! It's read differently, more linearly, and doesn't need glitz and gimmickry to keep the reader's attention. Unless you're publishing a gift book, think clean, simple, functional.

For designing your pages, a fancy page layout program might be nice, but in most cases it's not at all necessary. A word processor will usually do the job. My own tool of choice is Microsoft Word. I do have Adobe InDesign as well, and I use it on literary novels and on books with complex layouts or numerous graphics. But I prefer Word for most of my books, because it makes it easier for me to revise the writing during and after formatting.

Your choice of software, though, is less important than knowing what to do with it. The time-honored way to learn book design is to copy elements of books you admire. Look at things like font, line length, space between lines, margins, headings, headers, footers, and ornaments. You don't need to follow just one book's design—mix and match as you like.

You'll also want to take note of the book's parts—title page, copyright page, dedication, chapters, appendix, and so on. A style manual like *The Chicago Manual of Style* will list all the common parts of a book and tell you the order they should appear in, and some self publishing guides will too. One that does it particularly well is Jennifer Basye Sander's *The Complete Idiot's Guide to Self-Publishing.*

Keep in mind that most parts of the book usually begin on odd-numbered pages, which are always on the right-hand side! These pages generally do not include any header. Also, blank pages should be *completely* blank, with no header or footer. (Tip: In a word processor, set up the entire book in a single file but define chapters and other parts as separate *sections,* setting the properties of each section's first page.)

To emphasize words, you should always use italics instead of underlining. And always use print punctuation like "curly quotes" (', ', ", ") and true dashes (—) instead of plain-text punctuation like straight quotes (', ") and double hyphens (--). Some programs, like Word, can substitute the proper characters automatically, depending on your settings.

Between sentences, type one space only, never two. In almost all cases, use proper indented paragraphs *without* extra vertical space between. Of course, you should make sure your text is *justified,* with even edges at the left and right margins. Set your program to avoid *widows* and *orphans*—isolated lines at the top or bottom of the page.

A common mistake is to simply use your program's default font, such as Times New Roman from earlier versions of Word and InDesign. The narrow characters of this font were designed for newspaper columns, so they're completely wrong for the longer lines of type in most books.

A much better choice is a traditional book font such as Palatino, Garamond, Baskerville, Century Schoolbook, or Sabon. A favorite font of mine is Georgia, which comes from Microsoft and was specially designed for the Web. It's particularly well suited to the vagaries of both word processors and print on demand, and it's exceptionally readable at normal sizes. (But this quality may make some critics mistake it for "large type"—so you might want to set it at a size one point smaller than you'd use for other fonts.)

Even if you've worked with one or more editors, you'll have to proofread your finished text carefully, and hopefully find others to do it too—or better yet, hire a professional proofreader. Whatever you do, don't try to palm off the job on your spelling checker. Sure, you should use a spelling checker to help find misspelled words—but it can't tell you if a properly spelled word is in the wrong place, or if it's the wrong word entirely, or if the punctuation and spacing around it is correct!

For photos and illustrations not in color—and often for color ones too—a consumer-level "photo-paint program" is probably all you need. I highly recommend Adobe Photoshop Elements, which has fewer features than the professional Photoshop but inherits all its legendary quality.

But here too, the program you use is less important than knowing what to do with it. If you don't have experience in photo editing, take the time to read a basic book on it. You'll be amazed at how dramatically most images can be improved in a few simple steps.

You'll want to learn too about different file formats and types of file compression for photo-paint images. In general, avoid using GIFs or JPEGs, with their formats almost synonymous with degraded graphics and low resolution. If you do want to use a JPEG file, make sure it has always been saved with settings for large image size and maximum quality. Otherwise, work with TIFF files, with either highest-quality JPEG compression or, better yet, a lossless compression method like LZW or Zip.

The standard resolution for photo-paint images meant for print is 300 ppi (pixels per inch) for photos and paintings and such, and 600 ppi for line drawings on POD presses. Higher resolutions won't increase quality, and lower resolutions—such as the 72 ppi you find in most Web graphics—will make the art look blocky.

If your book needs charts, diagrams, or other kinds of simple geometric drawings, you can often create them right in your word processor or page layout program. If not, your best choice is a "draw program" like Microsoft Visio—best for importing into Word for Windows—or Adobe Illustrator. Such drawings are a different kind of graphic that's not defined by resolution.

Depending on your POD service, you may be able to submit your final pages in various forms. For instance, your service may accept word processor files, or printed pages for scanning. But for general convenience, flexibility, and reliability, the preferred way is to submit your files in PDF—Adobe's "Portable Document Format."

Unfortunately, creating PDF files is not as straightforward as you might think. Yes, a file created from free software or by using the export command of a word processor might work fine for desktop viewing or printing. But that same file might fail completely on a commercial POD press—or be rejected by your POD service before it even gets that far.

Generally, you should not use any PDF creation software or export feature unless it has settings you can adjust to meet your POD service's requirements. Or if you just want to be as safe as possible, use Adobe Acrobat 4 or later. With Acrobat, you can create an acceptable PDF file from Word or just about any other program.*

---

* If your book has a simple layout, conventional fonts and characters, and no graphics or graphic effects, you can *probably* get away with using the PDF export feature in Word 2007—*if* you select the PDF/A option. For more on Word 2007 and PDF files, see the article on my Web site.

For an in-depth look at book design, I highly recommend James Felici's *The Complete Manual of Typography*. And if you're using Microsoft Word 2004 or earlier, be sure to see my own book *Perfect Pages*.

Craft Your Cover

We've already talked about the importance of your book title in bringing up the book in search results. We've talked about how it should also invite the customer to explore further. But for drawing attention in search results, nothing is more important than the book cover image.

Now, you may want your book to look as slick as anything you'd find on a bookstore shelf. But the truth is, most of those covers just don't work on Amazon.

That's because, when customers see your image, they don't see a cover of 6 x 9 inches, or 5 x 8, or 8½ x 11. Instead, they see one a bit shy of 1½ x 1½ inches—about twice the size of a postage stamp. Since your book probably isn't square, you may not get more than two-thirds of that! And if your book is in Amazon's Search Inside program, the Search Inside banner will normally squeeze the area by about another 20%.

Into this tiny space must fit everything you need to attract the customer—and it must be clear and recognizable. An impossible task? Clearly not, since we see attractive postage stamps all the time. But creating them is an art in itself. And you must master that art to create an image that works well on Amazon.

So, what can you place on a cover that will show up well when the whole thing is reduced to such a size? Along with a colored background, there are about three elements you can comfortably fit. They are:

1. The title—*without* the subtitle.
2. The author name.
3. A single, bold graphic.

Note that this is the *most* you can fit—but each one of these is optional. If you can get down to two elements, or even one, then you're ahead. For instance, some of my book covers have had only a title and my name. Others have had only a graphic!

Obviously, none of these arrangements will look much like a cover you'd see in a bookstore—but why should they? Such covers are designed specifically to sell themselves when a book is picked up or displayed on a shelf. If you're aiming at Amazon, there's just no reason to imitate them.

Don't get me wrong: I'm *not* saying your cover doesn't need to be *attractive*. It should be as *attractive* as you can make it! But *attractive* does not equal *slick*. A cover with minimal elements can be just as pleasing—and often more striking—than a conventional one. That is, if you can adjust your idea of what a book "should" look like.

For the title, your type will be much more readable at this small size if you stick to capital letters, however poor a design choice that might otherwise be. You might also try rotating the entire line of type to a diagonal, so it runs from corner to corner instead of straight across. This can give extra room for enlarging the type.

Don't use just any graphic, or a graphic that merely represents what's in the book. Use a graphic that reaches out and grabs the customer. For instance, a face looking directly out from the cover is great for this. Remember, the primary aim of your cover is to get customers to click on it, or at least to read the accompanying title.

OK, I've been telling you how to design your front cover to present the optimum image on Amazon. But maybe this isn't how you want your book to look in real life. Maybe it wouldn't look to you enough like a "real book." It's certainly true that such covers may draw flak from critics who think they're experts on book design but who know little about online marketing.

If my guidelines don't sit well with you, there may be another solution. Just as I advised you to have a long and short subtitle for different situations, you might have a *real* cover for general use, and then a related but separate book cover *image* that you submit to Amazon to *replace* the real one. I'll talk later about producing and submitting such images.

Of course, you have more than just the front cover to deal with for your book. But if you're aiming at Amazon, the other areas aren't nearly as important. On Amazon, a customer is much less likely to flip the book over!

You'll want the book's title and your name on the *spine*—the edge you see when the book's on a shelf. On the back, you can put anything you like, or nothing at all. I especially advise you to leave off the price, which most books show there. Printing your price just makes it harder to change if you want to.

Eventually, your back cover will have a bar code so that the book can be identified mechanically. But almost any POD service will add that for you—and you should let it, because bar codes can be a hassle and can get fouled up surprisingly easily. Note, though, that a *bar code* is not the same as an *ISBN*, which is the number encoded *in* the bar code. Most POD services will provide an ISBN to go *with* the bar code, but Lightning Source, for example, will not.

The other thing to remember about the bar code is that the book price too is often encoded in it. If you don't want your price printed, make sure it doesn't go into the bar code either.

You can design your cover in almost any software you can think of—yes, even in Microsoft Word, as I managed to do as an experiment for the cover of *Perfect Pages*. You'll get best results, though, if you use a professional page layout or illustration program and follow your POD service's recommendations as closely as possible. I personally enjoy creating my covers in

Adobe InDesign, sending the result through Adobe Acrobat for the PDF file.

Common wisdom is that cover graphics are supposed to be composed in professional software like Adobe Photoshop so you can work in a special color mode called CMYK. This is meant to provide greater color accuracy on the press. Frankly, this is wasted on POD, where colors are never that exact and will vary over time. In most cases, a consumer-level program like Photoshop Elements will do just fine. If your POD service insists on CMYK images, Acrobat Pro can convert the color on or after the creation of your PDF file. But usually your images will be accepted either way, even if CMYK is officially required.

The special ink used in many of today's POD color presses can cause problems on a cover when laid on too thickly in multiple layers, as can happen with darker colors. In fact, exceeding a POD print service's recommended "total ink limit"—commonly no higher than for newsprint—can cause your cover to be rejected. It should be OK to have small areas of such color, but avoid big blocks of it in images or background.

If the prospect of preparing the cover intimidates you, then you can make things easy on yourself and hire a professional designer—as long as you make clear what your cover will need to work on Amazon. For starters, have your designer go over what you've just read here. I know that some of my readers have done just that, and that their designers thanked them for it!

Stick to a Format

Self publishers are sometimes tempted to add an alternate format to their standard, paperback one—maybe a hardcover version, or a large-print edition, or even an ebook. But if you're aiming at Amazon, don't do it. It breaks one of the cardinal rules of maximizing Amazon sales: *Stick to one format.*

Here's the reasoning behind the rule. On Amazon, the better your book sells, the more prominent it becomes in search results and other kinds of listings. And as that happens, the better it sells. It's a self-feeding cycle, and it's exponential. The catch is that this generally applies to each format *separately.* If your sales are split between two formats, those sales won't take your book as far, either in the separate formats or together.

Another reason is that Amazon will normally feature only one format of a book in search results, and you can't control which one. Among print formats, it's generally the one that has any copy on sale at the lowest price, which is usually the paperback—but you can't count on that, because Amazon looks also at the price of used copies from third-party vendors. And if it's the hardcover that's prominent, the customer may not realize there's a paperback too and may be discouraged by the higher price for new copies.

In another instance, if you've published your book both in print and as a Kindle Book, Amazon may decide to push the Kindle version. And if so, the customer may not realize there's even a print version available.

There's only one way to entirely prevent such complications: Give Amazon only one format to show.

Collect Comments

Nothing sells a book like other people's good opinions of it. On Amazon, this function is mostly served by customer reviews, but you should kick start the process by assembling a good collection of testimonials and/or media reviews. With *The Business of Writing for Children,* one reason for its success was that I managed to get great comments from almost twenty authors, editors, and such, many of them with names easily recognizable in the children's book world.

A good time to solicit testimonials is when your designed pages are ready for proofreading. At that time, email every respected person you know in the field or the genre and ask if they'd be willing to comment on a PDF file of the book. Tell them that you'd like just one to three sentences. You really don't want more, though you'll often get it anyway!

Tell them exactly how and where you intend to use their comments. Also let them know how long they can have to send them. This should be a fairly short time, like a couple of weeks. With a longer period, your book will most often be set aside and forgotten. Keep in mind they only have to read enough of the book to get a feel for it—and that's usually all they'll do.

Finally, tell them you'd like to send them a copy of the printed book later, whether or not they've commented. Include any physical address you already have for them, so they can make sure it's current.

If they reply with an offer to comment, send them your PDF file as an email attachment, or provide a link to download it. Make sure you've made the file as small as possible, with any graphics tightly compressed or removed. Remind them of the desired comment length and the deadline, and ask them to include exactly how they wish to be identified, with name and description.

A few days before the deadline, send a reminder and ask if they've had a chance yet to look at the book. This is often just what it takes to shake them loose. If it doesn't work, you can send another such note when the deadline arrives. At this point you can say, if they're not ready to send a comment now, it will be too late to include with the book, but they can still send one for you to include with promotional materials.

Later, when the book is printed, be sure to get it quickly to everyone you contacted. If they didn't comment earlier, mention that they can still send you a comment for promo materials—or if the book is already listed on Amazon, they can submit a customer review there.

If you don't personally know a lot of impressive people in your field or genre, there are still ways to get testimonials. When I wrote *Books, Typography, and Microsoft Word*—the ebook that later grew into my book *Perfect Pages*—I asked on several email discussion lists for comments on preliminary drafts. Not only did I get good suggestions for the book, I also got what I wanted even more: praise that I could use as testimonials. Whenever I received such a comment, I simply asked the writer if I could use it in promotion. I don't believe I was ever turned down.

Unfortunately, when I worked on *Perfect Pages* itself, I made a mistake you can learn from. Instead of posting the whole text together, I posted it chapter by chapter over a period of a couple of weeks. I thought that would give me more mileage. Instead, very few people got through all the chapters, so I received *no* overall comments from it that I could use in promotion.

Testimonials can be used in several places. I usually add mine on unnumbered pages at the beginning of the book. (You can do that by defining those pages as a separate section in your document.) At least some comments could be placed on the cover instead, but putting them all inside seems easier to me—or at least less worrisome, in reducing the risk of prominent errors or glaring typographic compromises.

Next I post the testimonials on my Web site. And of course, finally, I post them on Amazon itself, in the book "content" I can submit as a publisher. (I'll explain that later.)

Comments in testimonials or reviews often come in a very rough form, and almost all can use at least a little editing. The basic rule in editing a comment is that you cannot change the meaning. But it's always fine to shorten it, and you usually need to—if for no other reason, to rid it of excess words. For instance,

> Shepard's book *Aiming at Amazon* is amazing in my opinion.

becomes

> Amazing.

You're allowed to remove words and phrases without calling attention to it, but if you take a big chunk out of the middle, it's common to insert an ellipsis.

> I asked my wife what she thought of the book. But she was holding the baby, and she said she couldn't put it down.

becomes

> I asked my wife what she thought of the book. . . . She said she couldn't put it down.

(Just kidding. Don't change the meaning!)

If the commenter does something odd like addressing you directly, it's OK to substitute a word or phrase with another one in brackets. For instance,

> I read your whole book in one sitting.

becomes

> I read [the] whole book in one sitting.

If you need to significantly change the way a commenter is identified from the way they requested—for instance, in order to make their identification consistent in style with others—it's usually best to get approval.

Gathering testimonials and reviews is a long-term process, starting when your book is first in presentable form, and continuing long after publication. If you think a comment can help your book, don't let it get away!

3
Accessing Amazon

Set Up Accounts

Most readers of this book will already have a customer account on Amazon.com, Amazon's U.S. site. You'll need *at least* one account to market your book there—and you may well want more. (If you have an account on Amazon in Canada, the U.K., France, or Germany, it will work for the U.S. too.)

If you *don't* have one, starting one is quick and easy, from within the U.S. or anywhere else in the world. Go to

www.amazon.com

Click the new customer "Start here" link at the top of the page. All you'll need to supply for now is your email address, your name, and a password. You do not need to buy anything to start an account.

For marketing, it's often useful to have *more* than one account. For instance, I have an "Aaron Shepard" account, plus another under an earlier name that appears on several of my books. I use these accounts for marketing in my role as author. I also have a "Shepard Publications" account for when I approach Amazon as a publisher. Each of my accounts has a different email address clearly derived from the name I use on the account.

You can also have more than one account with the same email address, just by using different names. In fact, you can have the same email address *and* the same name on more than one account, just by changing the password. This might be useful, for example, if you want a public account as an author and a private one as a regular customer. Your readers would then be less likely to discover your odd passion for electric can openers, or your illicit interest in garden gnomes.

To add another account, first sign out of your active one. To do that, look at any page top for the link to click if you're not who Amazon thinks you are. This will bring you to the sign-up page. If you're using the same email address as before, you must still also choose the "new customer" option.

If you change your mind, just sign back into your existing account, or ignore the form entirely and navigate to another page. In that case, Amazon will just wait till the next time it needs to know who you are, then ask you again to sign in.

Once you have multiple accounts, you can sign in and out of them as you like, using the links at the page tops. There may also be times when you prefer to browse the site while not signed into *any* account. Amazon customizes the site based on your viewing and purchasing history, and you might want to check what is shown to customers with no history at all.

Though you don't need to buy anything to start an account, you *will* need at least one account with which you've made at least one purchase—and it has to be from Amazon in the U.S. That's what Amazon.com requires for access to a number of its social features, such as commenting on reviews, suggesting tags, and uploading Customer Images. Just make sure you're signed into such an account when you try to access those features.

Of course, most people pay Amazon by credit card, but you can instead pay by check or money order. One restriction is that any one credit card can be used only on one account. That's mostly to discourage authors from opening multiple accounts for spamming—a serious problem that has thankfully at least been scaled back.

If you're outside the U.S., a credit card should pay for your Amazon.com purchase from anywhere in the world. You can even avoid the cost of international shipping by buying something for a friend in the States!

Find Resources

As we go along, I'll give you Web and email addresses for obtaining details on various Amazon features. But one centralized resource you should know about is the Publishers and Book Sellers Guide, useful to both publishers and authors.

www.amazon.com/publishers

Most of the important info you'll find there—and more—is covered in this book. But you might still want to check there for helpful details and updates, or for completely new features.

If you hear of a feature that's not covered in this book *or* in the Publishers Guide, you can try searching in Amazon's Help pages. Or you might try a shortcut. You see, Web addresses on Amazon tend to be a bit convoluted, so key pages are often given a shortcut address as well. For instance, here's the Publishers Guide address replaced by the shortcut above.

www.amazon.com/gp/help/customer/display.html?
nodeId=13685551

Not so easy to type!

But how do you find a shortcut? Sometimes Amazon will reveal it in Help pages or email correspondence—but often, as in the example above, they're simple enough to guess. In fact, that's where a lot of the Web addresses in this book came from! Just start with

www.amazon.com/

and add a key word or phrase to the end, in lower case with no spaces. It's always fun when you hit the jackpot.

Make Contact

Amazon provides a special access point for authors who want to communicate with it: Author Central. Since you need at least one book listed on Amazon before enrolling, I'll wait till the next chapter to discuss it fully. But for now, here's the address.

authorcentral.amazon.com

To reach a contact form, click on the "Contact Us" link on any Author Central page, or go directly to

authorcentral.amazon.com/gp/help/contact-us

A more general access point for Amazon is its General Questions contact form. You can reach it with the "Contact Us" button found on every Help page. Or use this direct address.

**www.amazon.com/gp/help/contact-us/
general-questions.html**

By choosing the subject "Other Questions and Comments," you can use this form for just about any issue you want. Among this form's advanced features is an option to request a call-back for phone contact.

A more limited but still broadly useful gateway is the Features and Services contact form at

**www.amazon.com/gp/help/contact-us/
features-and-services.html**

Among the features this form addresses are the many interactive programs—Customer Reviews, Your Profile, and so on—

that Amazon places under the umbrella label of "Community." Choose the desired feature with the pull-down subject menu.

Though I don't recommend using this next contact form, I'll mention it in case you get desperate: the form for Amazon Advantage. At least one self publisher got help through this form even though he was not signed up for the program! Find the link at

advantage.amazon.com

or go direct to

http://advantage.amazon.com/gp/vendor/ public/contactusapp

With any of these contact forms, be as specific as you can. If asking about a particular book or books, be sure to identify each by both its title and its ISBN or ASIN. (I'll explain those terms in the next chapter, if you don't know what they mean.)

Keep in mind that messages sent through these contact forms go to someone in Customer Service, who is often *not* the one who can ultimately act on your request. Your success, then, will often depend on how well the receiving customer service agent is able to understand your inquiry, redirect it, and act as intermediary. With the General Questions contact form, you might want to spell out in your message the name of the department that should handle it—or if you don't know the name, identify it by its job. For instance, if you're writing about a book listing, you might ask to have your message forwarded to the Book Catalog Department. Or you could do this in a follow-up message, if Customer Service doesn't seem to know quite how to deal with you.

Often your initial message will reach someone who does not even really read it. They simply skim it to figure out what typical question you're asking or what common stupid mistake you're making. Then they send you a form message that deals with what they assume you said.

The problem, of course, is that you may have said something completely different. Instead of throwing up your hands in disgust and just bearing with incompetence, respond patiently, quote the previous correspondence, explain that you meant something different, and go over it all again. Often, these follow-ups are bumped up to the next level of agent, where they're handled with more expertise. In any case, I've found that my second tries are read much more carefully and are generally dealt with to my satisfaction, if at all possible.

Many of Amazon's departments also have their own email addresses for inquiries, and I'll give you many of them as we go along. (Unfortunately, the all-important Book Catalog Department is no longer among them.) There's also a general email address for the same Community features handled by the Features and Services contact form.

Community-Help@amazon.com

Look Up Your Profile

You'll be contributing a number of different kinds of content to Amazon, and I'll give you specific Web addresses to view and handle each kind. But you also have centralized access to many of them through your Amazon Profile, which Amazon sets up for all accounts. While logged in to your account, go to

www.amazon.com/gp/pdp

Later, I'll discuss Your Profile specifically as a marketing tool. For now, you should at least adjust the settings to make sure it doesn't show more than you want! To do that, just click on "Edit Your Profile." You can then tell Amazon to reveal different amounts of info to you, your Amazon Friends, and everyone else.

Keep Up with Change

Amazon changes rapidly. To avoid being left behind, figure on visiting the site at least once a week to spot new features and changes in old ones.

You can also get announcements of major developments through Amazon's news releases. Find them at

www.amazon.com/pr

There you can also sign up for email alerts of when new ones are posted.

Take the Express

One of the very best ways to access Amazon isn't on Amazon at all: my own Sales Rank Express. I'll often mention it in the pages ahead.

Sales Rank Express began as a private tool for checking sales ranks, then evolved into a free, public, multi-purpose tool for Amazon checking, analysis, and manipulation—a kind of Swiss Army knife for authors and publishers aiming at Amazon. Its main page, for example, includes handy links to all the Web addresses given in this chapter. Find it at

www.salesrankexpress.com

Documentation can be found in the Help/FAQ on the site. Read it to get the full benefit of this surprisingly versatile tool.

4
Marketing on Amazon

Check Your Listing

If you've optimized your book for Amazon in the ways I've advised, the book's success then depends on how Amazon displays it and what's displayed with it. That's what will attract customers and convince them to buy. So, most of this chapter is about improving and enhancing the presentation of your book.

Of course, before you can improve how your book is presented, you have to make sure it's listed in the first place! This may not happen quickly or all at once. A basic listing may appear within a few days after you approve a proof from your POD service. At that point, you should be able to find the page by searching on the book's ISBN, and within a few more days, by searching on title or author. But it may take a week or so from the page's first appearance before you see other parts— such as a description or a cover image.

In fact, if you're working directly with Lightning Source for the first time, the complete process can take up to a month. This isn't Lightning's fault—it's due to Ingram, which supplies some of the content Amazon displays. The delay is the time taken by Ingram to set you up as a publisher in its system. (After the first book, processing is much faster.)

Sometimes the searchability of a book gets hung up and doesn't extend to the author or title. If you can't search on those within a few days of your book's appearance on Amazon, let Amazon know. The most direct way is through the Search Feedback box at the bottom of any search results page, where you'll see "Did you find what you were looking for?" Click the "No" button, and a text box will open for your explanation. You can also try one of the contact methods discussed in the previous chapter.

And if your book never shows up at all? Contact Amazon, identifying your book and saying from what major suppliers it's available. (For most POD books, that's Lightning Source and Ingram.) Be prepared to decline any advice about joining Amazon Advantage to make sure your book is available.

As your book makes its way through the Amazon system, its availability too will evolve. At first your book may be shown as unavailable, then move to an availability of days or weeks. But by the time everything else is in place, it should show as "in stock" and orderable with "one-day shipping."

If your book is printed by Lightning Source, you may notice it's suddenly available not only from Amazon itself but also from a large number of third-party vendors selling through Amazon Marketplace—and often at prices lower than Amazon's. These vendors are not ripping you off. If a customer orders your book from them, they order it in turn from Ingram or even Lightning*—just as Amazon might—and you get your payment. And a sale by a third-party vendor is still counted toward your book's sales rank.

Over the years, Amazon has adopted various straightforward and predictable schemes of discounting a book based on its wholesale discount, sometimes along with the level of its cover price. Nowadays, though, the calculation seems more open-ended and flexible, apparently based on a multitude of factors. These include the book's wholesale discount, its cover price, whether the book is selling, how much it's selling, its search history, and more. In fact, there may be factors not even related to the individual book!

---

* Only one Marketplace vendor would be able to order directly from Lightning, namely The Book Depository, an international online bookseller I discuss in the appendix. With this privileged access, The Book Depository may be the first outside seller to offer your book on Amazon.

The upshot is that you can never really be sure how your book will be discounted, or whether it will be discounted at all. But typically, Amazon may apply a discount within a couple of weeks of the book's appearance, especially if the book has begun to sell. At this writing, a POD book at a standard wholesale discount might be discounted on Amazon between 20% and 30%, while a book at short discount is most often discounted 10%.

If your book is available *only* through *Amazon* POD, you probably won't see a discount at all. Why not? No competition! If Amazon's customers can't get a book anywhere else, Amazon sees much less reason to sell it for less.

An efficient way to keep tabs on the progress of your book listing is with Sales Rank Express. S.R.E. results will show all essential elements of that listing, including availability and discount, while prominently noting any missing elements.

Books at Amazon, as elsewhere in the book industry, are identified by ISBN—International Standard Book Number. This is the thirteen-digit number represented by the bar code on your book's back cover—the number that you either were given by your POD service or purchased from an official agency. Every format of every edition of every book is required to have a unique ISBN to distinguish it.

In Amazon's internal systems, though, it doesn't use that ISBN directly. Instead, it uses an *older* form of the ISBN, which has ten digits only. And actually, Amazon doesn't call it an ISBN at all, it calls it an ASIN—Amazon Standard Identification Number. (For a book *without* an ISBN, or for any item other than a book, Amazon simply creates an ASIN from a combination of letters and numerals.)

As an example, the ISBN of *Aiming at Amazon* is

978-0-938497-43-1

This can also be written without hyphens like so.

9780938497431

In the old ISBN-10 format, it would be

0-938497-43-X

or

093849743X

That last number—ten digits, no hyphens—is what Amazon uses for the ASIN.

How do you find your own book's ASIN? If you go to the book's Amazon page, you'll see the ten digits together in the Web page address displayed by your browser. Or scroll down the page to see that same number listed as the book's ISBN-10. You can also find the ASIN listed in results on Sales Rank Express. Or you can convert from the thirteen-digit ISBN to ISBN-10 with this handy form offered by the Library of Congress.

pcn.loc.gov/isbncnvt.html

Naturally, your book can be found by either its ASIN or its ISBN as soon as its page appears on Amazon—in fact, before you can successfully search for it by anything else. Just enter either number, with or without hyphens, in an Amazon search box—or use that number *without* hyphens to look up the book on Sales Rank Express to get a link. You can also swap your ASIN into the following Web address, currently set up for *Aiming at Amazon.*

www.amazon.com/dp/093849743X

On Amazon, *everything* related to your book—its ISBN, its title, all descriptive matter, reviews, tags, everything—is pegged to its ASIN. Basically, to Amazon, the book *is* the ASIN. In fact, Amazon doesn't even keep a static page for your book. Every time a customer wants to see the page, it's assembled fresh from the data associated with that ASIN.

Now, say you switch POD services and have to give the book a new ISBN. Amazon will then give it a new ASIN as well and treat it *as a new book with its own page*. Meanwhile, the old book with the old ASIN will continue to be listed and displayed. And, no, you cannot get that listing removed. Unless a book has been listed with the ISBN incorrect or missing, it's there to stay.

What if you want customer reviews, tags, and the like to be carried over from the old page to the new? For that, the books need to be *linked*. Often, Amazon will figure that out and link them automatically. In case it doesn't, I'll tell you soon how to make that happen.

Claim Your Book

Amazon wants to know you're an author and what books you've written. This helps Amazon set up a special Author Page on which customers can find all your books together and learn more about you. And you want Amazon to know for the same reasons—but also to make sure Amazon listens if there are problems with your book listings.

So, if this is your first book on Amazon—and even if it isn't, if you haven't done this already—your first task after seeing your new book listed is to head over to Author Central and sign up. That address again is

authorcentral.amazon.com

You'll be asked to identify the book or books you've written, and your request will then have to be approved by Amazon. If Amazon has any question about your status as the author, it may try to contact your publisher—which in this case is you! You can check the status of your account request by going to

**authorcentral.amazon.com/gp/help/
account-status**

Meanwhile, you'll have full access to Author Central, and Amazon will invite you to start setting up your Author Page—but anything you submit will be held up till your account is approved. (I'll talk later about setting up your page.)

If you've had books on Amazon for some time but are just now signing up for Author Central, you may find that Amazon already has an Author Page for you. In that case, signing up with Author Central should associate the existing Author Page with your new Author Central account.

Problems may arise, though, if Amazon has already created *more* than one Author Page for you. For instance, Amazon may have created separate Author Pages for the same name with variations—the difference of an initial, or the use of a nickname—or even for the name in exactly the same form. In that case, you can send a request to Author Central to "merge author names."

If the earlier Author Page you find on Amazon lists a book that shouldn't be there, you can contact Author Central and ask for its removal. But if it's really your book, it will probably stay. Amazon doesn't care, for instance, if the book is out of print.

If you were enrolled in the late, lamented AmazonConnect program, then everything in your AmazonConnect account should already have migrated to Author Central and be waiting there for you when you sign up.

If you write under more than one name, you could open more than one Author Central account by applying from different customer accounts—but you don't need to. Once you claim books written under separate names, Amazon should set up or assign separate Author Pages under the same Author Central account.

What you *can't* do very well is separate your books if you write in different genres under the *same* name. Though you *might* be able to set up more than one Author Central account and Author Page with the same author name—again, by starting from different customer accounts—this will in some cases just mean that the customer sees links to each Author Page side by side. So, there's really not much point.

If you already have an Author Central account when your new book appears on Amazon, then the first thing to do is go to Author Central to add it to your list of books. Click on the Books tab, then on the "Add more books" button. Amazon will automatically search on your name and show you all the possibilities it finds. If you don't see your new book, start a new search on its ISBN or ASIN (ISBN-10).

If the book's listing includes your name as Amazon knows it, your claim should then be accepted automatically. If not, you may be asked for a listing correction and then have to wait for acceptance. If you wrote the book under another name, Amazon will place it on a separate Author Page for that name, though you'll access that page from the same account.

Make Corrections

As mundane as it sounds, the most important thing you can do for your book on Amazon is to make sure it's not only listed but listed *correctly*. A single misspelling in the title or in your name can prevent customers from finding the book.

It's amazing how many publishers and self publishers neglect this. I know, because I sometimes find myself correcting title and author data for books I feel sorry for—including some books on self publishing!

The data received electronically from POD providers and wholesalers is copied automatically into Amazon's database, so there is little room for error on Amazon's part. If you do see a mistake, it probably originates farther upstream, so check and get it corrected back there.

There are times, though, when Amazon may have formatted the data oddly, or gotten the wrong name as publisher, or left off one of the contributors. Or when a Marketplace vendor may have carelessly entered your book in the system before Amazon received data from an official source. Or when you want Amazon to show different data entirely from what you gave your POD service.

To change the most basic data about your book—not including enhancements like the description or the cover image, which I'll talk about separately—you'll use Amazon's Catalog Update Form. This form shows you the current data for the book and invites you to enter your suggested changes.

There are several ways you can reach the form. One is through the "update product info" link in the light blue Feedback box near the bottom of your book's detail page. You can also reach it through your Author Central account. On the Books tab, click on any cover image or title, then on "Suggest product information updates." Or go to the form directly with an address like the one below for *Aiming at Amazon*. For a different book, just replace the ASIN (ISBN-10) at the end.

www.amazon.com/gp/gfix/welcome.html? ASIN=093849743X

Yet another handy way is through Sales Rank Express. Next to each book's listing in results is a "Fix Data" button that sends you to the form.

Whether or not you access the form through Author Central, *make sure you're signed into the same customer account you used to sign up for that*. This puts your corrections on a fast track to consideration and acceptance. In fact, it may be the only way they'd get made!

Author and contributor names should be entered first name *first*—as in "Arthur Author," not "Author, Arthur." And don't add anything after an author's name and separate it by a comma. Amazon will take the comma to mean the name is in inverted order and will move your suffix to the beginning—for instance, changing "Arthur Author, Jr." to "Jr. Arthur Author."

At times, Amazon may list the binding of a POD book as "Print on Demand." Of course, it is that, but that's not how you want it listed. The POD label still carries a stigma for some people, and others won't know what it means. So, if you see this designation, use the form to change the binding to "Paperback"—which is just as truthful and much more helpful.

One of the most important uses of the Catalog Update Form is to finally submit the long subtitle I had you work on so long ago. When your book's listing shows up, go to the update form to enter the complete title with long subtitle, separating the parts with a colon and space—just as Amazon will show them. The form will enforce Amazon's length limit by dropping anything beyond 200 characters, counting both spaces and punctuation.

As an example, for my book *The Business of Writing for Children,* here's what I would copy and paste into the box.

> The Business of Writing for Children: An Award-Winning Author's Tips on Writing Children's Books and Publishing Them, or How to Write, Publish, and Promote a Book for Kids

As with most online forms you'll use in publishing, you should avoid typing directly into this one. Instead, copy and paste info from a file on your computer that has been triple-checked for accuracy. Don't include any special characters like "curly quotes" and true dashes—use only "plain text." (Note the "straight quotes" in the example above.) The easiest way to do this is in a text editor like Notepad on Windows, or like TextEdit on the Mac, instead of in a word processor.

Besides safeguarding your own accuracy, increase the chances of Amazon's properly attending to each correction by submitting only one at a time. This doesn't mean waiting between corrections, though—you can submit the form again for the same book as many times as you like, with no delays.

Apart from correcting obvious errors, Amazon doesn't like to make suggested changes unless they're backed by some kind of authority—and that's good, since anyone at all can access the update form and suggest whatever they like.

As I said before, belonging to Author Central will likely establish your authority all by itself. The corrections form also lets you cite one or more authoritative Web pages that display the data you suggest. Such a page might even be on your own Web site. Don't give a page on a private site like Bowkerlink or Ingram's ipage, because Amazon's customer service agents will not be able to access it.

Be careful that your correction does not contradict text shown on the cover image. Amazon will likely reject that. (Of course, you can always change the cover image first—as I'll tell you how to do.)

With proper authority, your requested change may sail through, with the change made and email confirmation delivered sometimes within minutes. If there's some question, there may be a delay of up to a few days as your request gets closer scrutiny. You may also get a delay just because a book is new or a slow seller, since Amazon gives priority to corrections for more popular books.

If you get no response within a reasonable time, or if your request is turned down, you can try again. The request will almost surely go to a different employee, and that person may treat it differently. If that still doesn't work, contact Author Central, or try sending a message through the General Questions contact form, as discussed in the last chapter.

If you're notified that your suggestion *is* accepted, check back the next day to see if the change has been made properly. Often it has not, and you may even see new error introduced! If there are any problems, submit again.

If the correction you need cannot not handled by the form, submit it directly to Author Central. Go to the Books tab, click on a cover image or title, and then on "contact us." You'll be taken to a special contact form with your book already identified.

You can also try the "any other feedback" link in the Feedback box on your book's detail page. That will open a text box right in the Feedback box. When using that, the identifying info for your book will be sent automatically with your message. Still another possibility is the General Questions contact form, where you might specify the Book Catalog Department as the intended recipient.

By the way, do *not* try to use Amazon Advantage's Update Item Content form to change data for a book sold through normal POD channels, even if you're enrolled in Advantage as a publisher. That form is *only* for books selling through Advantage.

When you get your listing just the way you want it, don't assume it will stay that way forever. Glitches can cause Amazon to lose newer data, or it may pick up bits from sources you don't expect. Check your listing periodically to make sure it's as it should be. Sales Rank Express is an excellent tool for this kind of checking too.

Add Your Content

As soon as your book's listing appears on Amazon, you're able to enhance it with in-depth info about your book. At least some of this info should wind up in prime position on your book's detail page, where Amazon will include it under the obscure and misleading heading "Editorial Reviews." If Amazon already has some of this kind of content for your book, yours will be added to it, or in some cases replace it.

To submit yours, use the Books Content Update Form. (Don't confuse this with the *Catalog* Update Form you used in the previous section for corrections!) Find it at

www.amazon.com/add-content-books

or its more formal address

http://www.amazon.com/gp/content-form? product=books

It's also linked from the main page of Sales Rank Express.

The first page of the form will ask for detailed contact info. If you have formed your own publishing company—say, to work with Lightning Source directly—this is pretty straightforward. But you can also use the form as an "author" instead of a "publisher." In that case, where the form asks for it, just give the official publisher's name—for instance, the name of your self publishing company—then supply your own contact info for the rest.

The first page also asks for your book's ISBN so the form can connect with Amazon's listing for the book. Then at the bottom are three terribly important little boxes labeled "Additional ISBNs (Optional)."

With these boxes, Amazon is asking you if the content you're submitting should be posted for more than one version of the book. These might be different formats—say, if you published in both paperback and hardcover. Or they could be different editions, if your book was published in an earlier form—even by a different publisher or self publishing company.

But the importance of these boxes goes beyond that. By adding additional ISBNs, you tell Amazon to permanently *link* those versions within its catalog. This means they'll in many ways be treated as one book. For instance, all content you submit in the future for one will also be added to any linked version, without your having to say so. The same customer reviews and ratings will appear for both. And only one version will be featured in search results, with links to the rest.

There are pluses and minuses to linking editions, and I'll talk about those when I discuss updating your book. But if you have different *formats* of the *same* edition, you should definitely link them.

Normally, you would use this form for linking when you're submitting new content. But if you have no new content, you can still use it, by resubmitting *old* content to make the form go through. Or you can request linking without using the form at all, by contacting Amazon through one of the methods already described. Or you can just wait a while, since Amazon is likely to figure out the link on its own.

To check for the linking, just look on Amazon for the various signs I've mentioned. You can also check for it at Sales Rank Express. In S.R.E. results, only one of the versions will show up, and its info will include a listing of "Linked Versions." You'll also see a "Get Versions" button that will bring up info on all of them.

On the second page of the Books Content Update Form, you'll find fill-in boxes for a number of kinds of content. These include

- Book description—up to 300 words
- Publisher's comments—up to 1,000 words
- Author's comments—up to 1,000 words
- Author bio—up to 500 words
- Table of contents—up to 1,000 words
- Inside flap copy (for hardcovers)—up to 1,000 words
- Back cover copy—up to 1,000 words
- Reviews (or testimonials)—up to 500 words each
- Excerpt/first chapter—up to one chapter

Here's how the form works: All boxes always appear empty, whether or not Amazon has already collected content of these kinds. Still, the only boxes you fill in are those for which you have *new* content. For each filled-in box, if Amazon hasn't yet received that kind of content, it's simply added to the Editorial Reviews. If Amazon already *has* received that kind—from you or anyone else—your new content *replaces* the old. Meanwhile, any older content you *don't* replace remains untouched. All this happens for both that book and any book linked to it.

For instance, if your book's detail page already shows a description—maybe one you supplied to your POD service, or one you submitted previously through the form—and you submit a new one, Amazon should replace the old with the new. But if you leave the description box blank, the old description will remain.

The exception to this behavior is reviews. (That's "reviews" in the strict sense, not "Editorial Reviews.") The ones you put in the form's review boxes are just added, without replacing anything older. So, you can return to the form and add more as often as you like.

As with the Catalog Update Form used for corrections, you should type your material for this form offline, in plain text with no special characters, then copy and paste. Don't get spooked if a box looks too small—the pasted text will still go in.

Though some boxes accept very limited HTML format coding, you don't need it, and it may cause problems or even lead to your submission being rejected. Straight text will work fine, and the line breaks you enter while typing normally will separate your paragraphs as you intend. You probably won't *see* your paragraphs separated in the preview that Amazon displays for your final approval, but they'll show up correctly when they reach the book's detail page. Have faith!

There is no way to insert images, video, links, or anything else fancy. Web addresses, contact info, and the like are not allowed.

At this point, you're naturally thinking of filling in as many fields on the form as you can, to provide as much content as possible. But *don't do it!*

The problem is that Amazon will display only two content elements right on the book's detail page. To view the rest, the customer must visit *another* page through a link to "See all Editorial Reviews." That is, if Amazon displays a particular type of content at all. At times, for instance, Amazon has simply stopped showing all tables of contents.

Reviews get top priority in Amazon's placement, followed by the book description. So, say that you filled in every box on Amazon's form. All you would see on the book's detail page itself is two reviews!

You can't count on customers clicking any link—so you want to get the most content possible right on the book's detail page. The trick with the Books Content Update Form, then, is to load all your content into a minimum number of boxes.

Your exact approach may vary according to your book, the content you've developed for it, and more, but here's an example of how you might go about it.

1. No doubt, you've already submitted a book description to your POD service. Let this stand as one of the two content elements that Amazon displays on your book's detail page. Or, if it hasn't arrived and you don't think it will, enter the exact same description on the form.

2. Take everything else you have that will fit and enter it into the box for "publisher's comments." This can include a longer description, an author bio, a table of contents, a short excerpt, even reviews and testimonials—anything you want to show Amazon's customers. Don't forget an "Also by" list of any related books you've published! With a length limit of 1,000 words, 8,000 characters, you have a lot of room to play in. Yet collectively, this will all count as a single content element—the second one that Amazon displays on the book's detail page.

3. Place a long excerpt into the form's box for that. Since Amazon gives low priority to this element, there's no danger it will shove more important content off the book's detail page. And though most customers won't follow a link to see it, you'll have it there for those who will. In fact, you can increase the chance of that by inserting a notice at the bottom of your publisher's comments—something like, "For a book excerpt, please click below on 'See all Editorial Reviews.'"

4. *Ignore all other boxes.*

The outcome of this approach is that you should have up to 1,300 words of your very own, right there near the top of your book's detail page. That can be more than enough to convince a customer to buy your book, if they're going to be convinced at all.

One fly in the ointment, though, might come if your book gains attention from major reviewers that license content to Amazon. In that case, Amazon will itself add that content to Editorial Reviews, pushing your submissions off the page. There's nothing you can do about that—but good reviews from major reviewers do make a great consolation prize.

One ill effect you might suffer with *any* approach to content submission is mishandling by Amazon. Processing of this form was reliable while done directly by Amazon's Book Catalog Department. But since late 2008, the job has been outsourced overseas with sometimes disastrous results—for instance, a new description being added to the tail end of the one it was meant to replace, or multiple reviews merged into a single element with the sources omitted.

If something like this happens to you, contact Amazon through its General Questions contact form and try to get it fixed. But your best preventive measure is to submit your content just once, just the way you want it, then leave it alone— and that includes anything you supply to your POD service for Amazon to pick up. Don't come back and tinker with what's already displayed, if you can avoid it. Also, as I've already suggested, embed your reviews and testimonials within another element, rather than using the boxes meant for reviews.

Amazon's outsourcing of this form's handling has also meant that processing can be *slow*. You may have to wait a few weeks for your content to appear.

I mentioned before that you should *not* try to use Amazon Advantage's Update Item Content form to change data for a book sold through normal POD channels, even if you're enrolled as a publisher. That holds true also for adding this kind of content. Again, Advantage's form is *only* for books sold through Advantage.

Submit a Cover Image

When customers find your book online, they don't see the book's *cover,* they see the cover *image.* Next to your book's title/subtitle, this is your book's most important selling point on Amazon.

Your POD service will have a cover image sent to Amazon based on the cover you submitted, either processed from your cover file or scanned from the proof copy. Most often, that image is OK, but you may feel you can do a better job. You may also want an image posted faster than your service can make that happen. By producing your own image, you can submit it as soon as your book's listing appears, or replace your service's image when it does show up.

Though your cover image can simply be a picture of your cover, it doesn't have to be—as I said in my section on cover design. Your cover image can instead stand on its own as a simplified, bolder version of the book's cover, heavily optimized for online viewing at the small sizes found on Amazon. Even if your actual cover was designed with such viewing in mind, you can usually push the cover image even farther in this direction.

Amazon does require your image to represent the actual book, and customers expect that as well. But few are likely to object if you keep the basic cover concept and adjust the elements.

For instance, if you used both capital and lower case letters in your cover title, you might switch to all caps in your cover image. If you included your author name and a subtitle on your cover, you might simply leave them off the image. A graphic might be cropped more closely and made relatively larger. Cover elements can even be overlapped—for example, the graphic might impinge on the title, or vice versa.

For any vertical book, you can also gain display area simply by widening the cover image. Amazon fits these images into a standard allowable area of equal height and width—in other words, into a square. A wider cover image would display at the same height but take up more of the square. And an image that's a square itself would give you the maximum possible display area. This is the shape I use for my own cover images, and it has been used by Amazon itself for the ebooks it called Amazon Shorts.*

Be aware, with extreme design modifications, you do run some risk of having your image rejected. Cover images are checked by Amazon at least cursorily before being allowed into the system. But whatever you come up with might at least be worth trying to submit. And on Amazon, repeated tries often bring success.

It's handy to produce your cover image for Amazon to specs that will allow you to use the image in other places too. The following specs should be acceptable almost anywhere.

> Face-on view (not angled or "3D")
> No border
> JPEG format
> 72 ppi (or dpi) resolution
> 9 inches max. height or width (648 pixels @ 72 ppi)
> RGB color mode
> sRGB color space
> 24-bit color depth (8 bits per channel)

These specs are slightly different from what Amazon will give you. Amazon actually prefers a minimum of 1000 pixels in

---

* If you want to get really picky, the ideal shape changes slightly if a Search Inside banner will be applied. In that case, the ideal would be a cover slightly wider than it is high, at a ratio of 19:18.

the longest dimension—but anything down to 500 pixels is accepted, and as I said, these specs are for an image you can use *anywhere*. Likewise, Amazon will accept a TIFF instead of a JPEG, but that might not be true when submitting elsewhere.

Also, Amazon says "sRGB color mode"—but this is a simple inaccuracy that has persisted for over a decade. sRGB is one possible color *space* in RGB color *mode*. But you probably don't have to worry much about all that. If you use a consumer-level graphics program, you should get the needed RGB color mode, sRGB color space, and 24-bit color depth, all by default. (And if you're using a professional-level program, I doubt you need me to explain all this to you.)

If the background is white or nearly so, Amazon invites you to ignore the "no border" guideline and surround the image with a thin black border or a thicker gray one. If you don't, your book will blend into Amazon's Web pages so it won't look like a book at all—and customers won't be sure where to click. (On the other hand, if you *want* that effect . . . .)

Be sure your JPEG is saved at settings for highest quality or lowest compression—two ways of saying the same thing. JPEG compression makes type blurry, and Amazon applies a good deal of it in its own processing—but at least you can make sure your image is as distinct as possible before Amazon gets its hands on it.

The image file should be named with the ISBN (without hyphens or spaces) and the file type extension. For instance, the image file for *Aiming at Amazon* is named

9780938497431.jpg

To check Amazon's own stated image guidelines, go to

www.amazon.com/images

If you like, you can test how well your image will stand up on Amazon. Reduce your image to 115 pixels maximum height and width—or whatever size Amazon presently uses for new images in search results—and save with about 50% ("medium") JPEG compression. You may then find that some color combinations don't look as good as others. For instance, black type on a dark red background can cause trouble.

Amazon used to provide convenient upload for cover images at a dedicated public drop point that was accessed by FTP, a fast and efficient way to send files over the Internet. Sadly, this was shut down, leaving self publishers scrambling for other ways in.

At this point, the only reliable option still open is through—*gasp*—Amazon Advantage. Now, you may recall that I specifically advised you *not* to sell books through this program—and I'm not saying any different now. But it's now possible to sign up for an Advantage account *without* enrolling your books. That way, Amazon will keep buying your books through other channels, while you will be able to upload a cover image whenever you like.

The address again for Advantage is

advantage.amazon.com

Once enrolled and signed in, look for an "Image Upload" link on the main page or on the Items tab. That will bring you to a simple Web form for uploading one image at a time.

One nice thing about submitting through the Advantage form is that it provides status reports and error messages, so you can check how your image is doing and fix problems. In fact, be sure to click through to the status report about a minute after submitting an image, to make sure it hasn't already been rejected! (If it's OK so far, you'll see "Processing." If you're checking too soon, you'll see "Pending.")

At times, you may find that your cover image needs to be resubmitted. For example, if you get an image posted and then the one from your POD service arrives, that one will likely replace yours till you can send it again. Also, if you have an older book on Amazon, you might find that its cover image seems stuck at a size smaller than normal. You can fix it by either submitting a new image or resubmitting the old.

If you submit an image twice through Advantage, though, you'll find that sending the exact same file is not allowed, because Amazon assumes it's an error. The solution is to tinker with the file in any way affecting size—for instance, generate a new JPEG with a slightly different amount of compression, or send a TIFF instead.

Share Other Images

While Amazon has been busily making it harder for self publishers to submit cover images, it has been making it extremely easy for anyone at all to share other images related to a book. This is done through the feature called Customer Images.

Thumbnails of up to four or five submitted images are shown on the book detail page, right below the cover image. Move your cursor over a thumbnail, and the associated image will take the place of that cover image. If you then click on either that replacement image or a thumbnail—or on the link "See all customer images"—you'll call up a "product image gallery" with larger versions of all available images, including any not seen on the detail page.

This is a fine way to show off photos or other illustrations from your book, or to display an author photo. Pages of text can also be displayed—though because of the small image size, they may not be legible unless you trim the margins and/or split the page vertically into halves. (I've used this to show tables of contents and sample pages from play scripts.) Customer Images can also be used to post an "interim" book cover image, which Amazon will display in that place till a "real" one arrives.

To submit an image, you must be logged in to an account from which you have made a purchase. Then just click the "Share . . ." link below the book's cover image and use the Web form to upload. Any typical JPEG file can be submitted, as long as you own the image rights. As with book cover images, a square will give you the biggest display area. You can add a caption and also add notes that appear when a cursor moves over specific parts of the image.

Up to five images can be uploaded through the form in a single batch, and you can return to the form as often as you like. Keep in mind that newer customer images are placed first—so, if you want yours to appear in a certain order, *reverse that order when uploading.*

If you want to make changes or delete, you can do that anytime, as long as you're logged into the same account. Simply go back to the book detail page or the image gallery and click on the image, or else access it through the Customer Images link in your Amazon Profile.

Tip: If someone else adds images after you and pushes your thumbnails off the detail page, just delete your old images and submit them again. That will move your thumbnails to the front.

For more detail on Customer Images, go to

**www.amazon.com/gp/customer-images/
customer-image-guidelines.html**

Consider Inside Search

Amazon's optional program of Search Inside lets customers browse through some of your book's pages online and search the entire text for specific content. It also lets Amazon access that text for normal searches, so that the book comes up more often in search results. Amazon also analyzes the text so it can suggest the book to customers when they look at related ones.

Many Amazon customers depend on Search Inside in deciding whether to buy a book. For nonfiction, it can help them see how well you address their needs. For fiction, it can help them decide if they like your writing style. For a book heavy on graphics, it can help them check quality, helpfulness, or appeal.

Details on the program are at

www.amazon.com/searchinside

or

www.amazon.com/sitb

You can also write to

InsideTheBook-Submission@amazon.com

or

InsideTheBook-Submissions@amazon.com

Originally, books were submitted to Search Inside in printed form, but Amazon now wants only PDF files, which are more convenient and yield images of higher quality. Amazon wants the entire book, with no omissions. Generally, you can send the same interior file you used for printing. Cover images and any other images with text should be at least 300 ppi to enable text recognition.

In most cases, you'll upload your files through Amazon's Seller Central—a site normally used by Marketplace vendors—where you'll get a special account just for Search Inside. It's at

sellercentral.amazon.com

Once logged in, look for the "PDF & Cover Upload" link to bring you to the Web form. If you have extremely large files or large batches, you can ask the Search Inside people to let you upload by FTP instead.

Files are generally processed within one to a few weeks. Amazon itself chooses the sample pages to feature—but once the book is online, you can request a different set. In the past, Amazon has also allowed publishers to request omission of specific pages from searching—for instance, cookbook pages with menus. At this writing, that option is not available, but it's expected to be restored in the future.

OK, I've said some nice things about Search Inside. So, it may surprise you that I do *not* advise you to use it.

This position has been one of the more controversial I'm known for, so let me go into some detail. I was probably one of the first self publishers to enter this program, and also probably one of the first to leave it. I initially found it very exciting, and I still feel it gives real benefits—but to me they are all overshadowed by one overriding consideration: Cover images are reduced in size so a "Look Inside" banner can fit at the top.

For example, at this writing, Search Inside cover images in search results are most often reduced in area by about a fifth.* As important as those images are to my publishing strategy, this is a deal breaker. I don't believe the program can bring me enough extra sales to offset the handicap.

The advantages of Search Inside are real and significant—but they do tend to be overstated by its supporters. In practice, the program's strengths can be counterbalanced not only by the cover image problem but by several other factors.

• Though allowing customers to see inside the book can definitely earn you some sales, it can also make a purchase unnecessary if the customer locates just the info they need. Also, the feature may satisfy customers who might otherwise buy the book partly from curiosity.

• Search Inside is helpful in relaying what's in the book, but you can do this also with the publisher content you submit through the Books Content Update Form and with Customer Images.

• Search Inside may bring up your book more often in search results, but except in highly specialized searches, it will generally be too far down the list to be noticed.

• While Search Inside can help Amazon draw customers from related books to yours, it can also help Amazon draw customers from yours to those others.

• Amazon delights in extracting and displaying all kinds of material from Search Inside text. Personally, I find this frivolous and distracting, and I'd rather they not do it with my books.

You may often come across mentions of a report by Amazon saying that Search Inside books showed a sales increase of

---

* The banner currently takes up 10% of the available height and 5% of the available width. For a book taller than it is wide, this means a forced 19% reduction in area. For a book wider than it is tall, the reducation is 10%. These figures are actually a great improvement. At the time I withdrew from the program, the reduction ranged between one-quarter and three-quarters!

around 10%. But this was from the very early days of the program, before everyone jumped on the bandwagon, and it may not have been for books taking advantage of other features. In any case, my own more recent experience would not support such a claim. Though such factors are hard to isolate, I didn't notice any loss of sales for books withdrawn from Search Inside.

In the end, of course, it's your call. Neither a decision for nor one against is likely to decide the fate of your books. And if you do sign them up then change your mind, you should be able to withdraw them individually or together just by writing to the program. The Search Inside agreement does stipulate a minimum time for a processed book to be included, but in practice, I found that a direct request for removal was honored regardless. The banner is then automatically removed from your cover images, with no need to resubmit them.

Amazon will eventually figure out, when almost all new books feature Search Inside, there's no point in taking up display space with a banner. At that point, I'll rejoin!

Suggest Tags

Tags are a relatively new feature on Amazon, but it has gone into them in a big way. Borrowing the idea from social networking sites, Amazon now uses them as an alternate means for customers to discover books—but that's not all. Tags now also feed into normal search results, pairings, and recommendations. So, despite their modest appearance, their effect is far-reaching on Amazon.

Tags for public view can be added by any Amazon customer, which of course includes you when signed into an account you've used for a purchase. (With any other account, you can still add tags, but they're *private*, seen by no one else.) Each customer can apply up to fifteen per book. The more times a specific tag is applied to a book, the more likely Amazon will display that book to customers searching on that tag.

A selection of the book's tags—up to eleven—are shown in a special section on the book's detail page, with a link to a complete list. In both locations, the tags are listed in order of popularity—or in alphabetical order when there's a tie—with the number of customers who applied each tag appearing next to it in parentheses.

Also in the tag section of the detail page are forms and links to add and manage your own tags. Using the forms, you can enter a number of tags together by separating them with commas—but the "quick" form won't accept more than 128 characters at a time and will leave off the end of the last tag if you go over. If a tag you enter is a duplicate of someone else's, your "vote" is added to it. If it's a duplicate of one of your own, it's discarded.

Upper case is ignored, while most punctuation, such as an apostrophe, is replaced by a space or just omitted. You're allowed to place a hyphen between words—but due to a quirk, Amazon will match the phrase in more cases if you instead leave a space.

Another easy way to enter a duplicate tag is to just click the checkbox next to one of the tags already displayed on the detail page—and that's what many people do, especially for the top tags listed. For this reason, it's worth your while to be the *first* to submit tags, so at least some of yours will be positioned where others will see them and are likely to second them. (To keep Amazon from moving *any* of your tags to another page, you may have to limit yourself to just a few.)

Here are some kinds of tags that may benefit you.

• Your author name.

• Key words and phrases from your title.

• Key words and phrases you couldn't fit into your title.

• For nonfiction, subtopics that might be of special interest to some readers. These might include personalities or locations or anything else with a smaller but still substantial presence in the book.

• For fiction, elements of the novel. For instance, any real-life location you used, or the profession or avocation of the main character.

• For a collection or anthology, key words and phrases identifying pieces of your book.

• Alternate spellings or common misspellings for any of the above.

Keep in mind that you're not tagging your book primarily to *describe* it to customers but to increase the number of tags it shares with similar books. That way, Amazon is more likely to display or recommend your book when the other books are displayed or purchased. For this purpose, tag with common words and short phrases that others too might apply. For example, the tag "a unique and inspiring view of osteoporosis" would be useless, because no one else would ever come up with it. What you'd want is a simple "osteoporosis."

You can access your tags for *all* books through the "Your tags" link on any book detail page, through your Amazon Profile, or directly at

www.amazon.com/gp/tagging/manage-tags

For help or info, write to

Tags-Feedback@amazon.com

By the way, if you go to add your tags to a new book and find a substantial list already there, don't be fooled. Read carefully how Amazon describes the list, and you may find they're only tags from "similar products." In other words, these are Amazon's best guesses, which will be removed as soon as any real tags are applied.

Along with its general-purpose tags, Amazon lets you add up to ten "Tags for Amazon Search." These directly cause a book to appear in Amazon searches on suggested terms.

Search tags are actually the older of the two varieties, starting life under the name "Search Suggestions." Amazon decided to deemphasize them in favor of general-purpose tags, but for now at least, the feature lives on with most of its original capability. The main access point to it is at the bottom of the tags section on each book detail page, where you'll find a couple of modest links for adding and managing search tags.

Most of the same key words and phrases you used as general-purpose tags can be repeated as tags for search. The main exception is that you're not allowed to use terms already in basic book data—title, author, and so on—which a search would find anyway. Also, the book must be directly relevant to a search on that term. This rules out, for instance, tagging with titles of your other books. (It also stops authors from abusing the system by tagging their books with *other* authors' book titles.) Only terms in English are accepted.

When entering your search tags, you don't have to worry about variations in punctuation and capitalization, because Amazon searches will ignore them. But word order does matter, so you can vary that to create different tags.

For each search tag, you must include an explanation of its relevance to the book. Though Amazon has stopped showing this explanation to customers, it is still carefully reviewed by Amazon staff—and if you're less than convincing, the search tag is rejected. One thing that helps is to embed the search tag itself into the explanation. For example, here is my explanation for tagging *Aiming at Amazon* with "book publicity."

> This book describes book publicity techniques for self publishers aiming at sales on Amazon.com.

Also required by Amazon is that the explanation tell something about the book itself. Here is an explanation that got my suggestion *rejected* when I tagged *Aiming at Amazon* with "Aaron Shepherd," a common misspelling.

> The book is by Aaron Shepard. (That's probably who you meant if you searched for 'Aaron Shepherd.')

And here's the revision that was later accepted.

> If you're looking for Aaron Shepherd or Aaron Shepard, this is his book on self publishing.

Search tags can be reviewed by Amazon within a day or so, then appear on the site within a few days. You can edit or delete them any time after submitting them—but if an accepted search tag is edited, it's reviewed by Amazon again. A rejected search tag will be "suspended," and you can try it again just by editing it—but you improve your chances if you delete it entirely and start over.

Besides the search tag links on book detail pages, a link to all your search tags can be found in your Amazon Profile—or while logged in, you can go to

**www.amazon.com/gp/associations/admin/
list-associations.html**

For more info, or to report abuse, you can write to the address given earlier for general-purpose tags, or try

Search-Suggestions-Support@amazon.com

Categorize Your Book

Each book on Amazon is categorized under a hierarchical scheme of Amazon's own. Making sure this is done correctly can be important in helping customers find your book.

When the categories are assigned, you'll find them displayed toward the bottom of your book's detail page under a heading like "Look for Similar Items by Category," with a link at each category level. Here, for example, is the listing for *Aiming at Amazon.*

Books > Business & Investing >
    Small Business & Entrepreneurship >
    Entrepreneurship
Books > Nonfiction > Social Sciences >
    Library & Information Science
Books > Reference > Publishing & Books >
    Authorship

Amazon's categories are mostly meant to help customers who like to browse by subject or to see bestseller lists, both of which choices are offered by the toolbar at the top of Amazon book pages. The more categories your book is assigned to, and the more relevant they are, the more likely such a customer will find you in an area of interest. Also, if your book places on a bestseller list—in other words, if it's in the top 100 books in any category, however specialized—the category and rank will be listed impressively on your book's detail page, right below the general sales rank.

If you don't feel Amazon has found all possible categories for your book, you can suggest others. To get ideas, look at the categories for similar books, and also search through the full list of choices. The best way to see this is through the Best-sellers feature. Again, reach it through the toolbar, or find it at

www.amazon.com/bestsellers

Amazon has no special online form for suggesting additions or changes in categories, so reaching the right people might need some persistence. Try Author Central, the "any other feedback" link on your book's detail page, and/or the General Questions contact form, maybe specifying the Book Catalog Department as the recipient. With luck, your suggestions will be forwarded to the right team, which then may or may not act on them.

In any case, be prepared to wait. At one point, Amazon reported that categories were updated only once a month, and one self publisher says a request can take up to six weeks. Of course, that's if it goes through at all. Morris Rosenthal reports once trying about monthly for half a year before achieving success.

Note that, before you suggest categories, you should wait till any descriptive content you're submitting through the Books Content Update Form has been posted. Amazon will use this content to evaluate your request.

Get Customer Reviews

Customer Reviews is the granddaddy of all Amazon special features and has established itself as one of the most powerful influences on book sales on Amazon. Because of that and its accessibility, it has also suffered more abuse by authors and small publishers than any other Amazon feature.

It's common to see reviews written by the author under phony names or, for older reviews, anonymously. Nowadays, Amazon tries to guard against fraud by posting reviews only from accounts from which a purchase has been made—normally meaning it's associated with a credit card—and also by encouraging the use of verifiable "Real Names." But some authors circumvent these measures by opening multiple accounts with different cards, or by using friends' accounts.

Equally common is to see reviews that the author solicited from friends who have no real interest in the subject but just wanted to "help out." For example, the earliest few reviews of a popular book on writing for children are by people who say they don't actually want to write for children!

Possibly even worse is the popular practice among authors and self publishers of writing reviews for the books of others only to plug their own, either within the review or in the byline—a kind of self-promotion that is prohibited by Amazon's participation guidelines and is grounds for a review's removal. And of course, the worst of all is to write negative reviews of competitors, or again, to have them written by "friends."

I don't do any of this. And I ask you not to do it either.

There's something about the Internet that can bring out the worst even in people who normally try to be ethical. People who would never think of cutting into a line or grabbing a taxi away from someone else will blithely steal sales by posting their advertisements on someone else's book detail page. I've even seen one popular manual on Amazon promotion take the trouble to euphemize this practice, calling it "competitive networking"!

Those who abuse Amazon's Customer Reviews are destroying the basis of trust that underlies their effectiveness. Already, many Amazon customers look askance at these reviews. This hurts all of us. And besides, is that really the way we want to behave?

I hope this book makes clear that you do not have to resort to deception or questionable practices of any kind to succeed on Amazon. These are usually desperate measures taken by people trying to make up for weaknesses in their books or in their marketing.

And guess what? Most of the time, these tricks don't work anyway. They seldom do more than make the author look amateurish—the same as all the other authors clawing their way over each other for a tiny slice of attention. As for the more extreme cases of fraud, they can be met with extreme reprisals, including Amazon's removal of *all* customer reviews, fraudulent or not, on *all* of an author's books.

So, do I simply leave customer reviews to take care of themselves? Not at all. I actively encourage them.

With all my books, I make myself easily accessible by including contact info. Then when anyone writes to thank or praise me, I reply—with their own comments quoted back to them—and ask them to consider posting a review on Amazon. To make it easy, I may also provide a link to that book's page for writing a review—like this one for *Aiming at Amazon*.

**www.amazon.com/review/create-review?
ASIN=093849743X**

This often brings back a note saying they'll be happy to write a review. I save this note for a few days, then reply with a brief note of thanks. The delay is so I can jog their memory if they mean to write the review but forgot about it. The reminder often prompts them to post the review before they can forget again.

I've also experimented with offering an incentive for reviews. For example, I publish a series of books on reader's theater, and I have an occasional email bulletin that teachers and librarians sign up for on my Web site. In the bulletin, I offered to send an ebook version of any of the reader's theater books to anyone who gave Amazon a customer review of one of them.

I was careful *not* to specify that the reviews had to be positive, though of course I figured they would be. After all, if the reviewers didn't like my work, why would they want an ebook of mine? Really, the campaign was merely an effort to get those who sincerely liked one of my books to express it on Amazon.

This campaign did generate some reviews, but I wasn't completely happy with the results. The main problem was that some of the reviewers had obviously not read the books, but were just looking for a freebie. I hadn't meant or wanted to generate reviews like that, both for ethical reasons and because those reviews just don't read as well. Also, one Amazon customer noticed the offer and wrote a customer review characterizing it as a bribe.

For these reasons, I've decided that incentives for reviewing—other than the standard free review copy—are generally a bad idea. Better to wait for reviews by readers who simply care enough about the book that they're willing to spread the word.

One common strategy for generating customer reviews is to solicit them from Amazon's "Top Reviewers"—customers recognized by Amazon for the multitude of reviews they write and for the number of "Helpful" votes given to those reviews by other customers. You can find a list of those reviewers at

www.amazon.com/review/top-reviewers.html

The list includes the reviewer's name, reviewer rank, and an excerpt from their Amazon Profile. From there you can click through to the complete profile or a collection of their reviews.

If you think a reviewer might be interested in your book, look in their profile for contact info, which most of these reviewers will provide there. Then send a message, offering a free review copy of your book with no expectations and no strings attached.

As an alternative, you can offer your book to numerous top reviewers and aspirants at once by posting a notice on the Customer Reviews Discussion Board at

**forums.prosperotechnologies.com/
am-custreview**

Again, make it clear that you're offering a free copy with no obligation.

You may have heard of Amazon Vine, a more high-profile method of soliciting Top Reviewers. In this program, Amazon distributes publishers' review copies to reviewers who request them. But Vine is open to larger publishers only, and besides, it costs a bundle—$5,000 plus miscellaneous charges, at last report. That's certainly much more than it's worth!

I have to admit, I have mixed feelings about dealing with Top Reviewers. Their little world has become rife with power plays, attention-grabbing, and back-scratching. In fact, it has spawned its own unique types of fraud and manipulation.*

There are certainly competent and sincere Top Reviewers, and Amazon has now altered its ratings system to reward quality as well as quantity. Still, the reviewers—many of whom seem to see themselves as God's gift to Amazon—often have no qualifications and little idea of what they're doing. At the same time, Amazon gives them prominence of place, so a horrendous review by one of them can wind up positioned ahead of all your book's other reviews—permanently.

You don't need Top Reviewers if you have done your homework and garnered a handful of testimonials from authoritative figures. And with nonfiction, this is seldom hard to do. Likewise, if you're a novelist with a few published friends, that should be enough to start you off. The only time I would reach out to Top Reviewers would be for fiction when I'd struck out with advance comments.

You might, though, use similar techniques to approach promising but less prominent reviewers. Look for high-quality reviews of books similar to yours, or even of earlier books of your own. The author of such a review might not show contact info on their profile, but you still might gather enough info from the review and/or the profile to locate that reviewer on the Web. You might also try sending an Amazon Friend invitation from the reviewer's profile page and customizing the message text—though the reviewer won't see the message unless they visit their own profile.

---

* For a fascinating discussion, see "Who Is Grady Harp?" by Garth Risk Hallberg, posted on Slate, Jan. 22, 2008.

Set Up Your Page

As I said before , your Author Page is where customers can find all your books and also learn more about you. At this writing, customers can reach that page through links in several places.

• On the author name listed on your book's detail page, below the book title.

• In a "More About the Author" section, also on the detail page, below the book's basic data.

• At the top of search results when they search on your name.

That doesn't mean a ton of customers will be visiting your page, but you want to get it ready for those who do. To do that, sign into your Author Central account. The address again is

authorcentral.amazon.com

Click the Profile tab. You'll see one button for adding or editing your bio, and another for uploading or changing your photo.

For your bio, Amazon wants something at least 25 words long, but really not more than a paragraph. Any paragraph breaks will be ignored, and if the paragraph gets long, Amazon will hide the last part of it behind a link. The author bio from your book or books will usually work well here. HTML code is not allowed, and neither is any personal contact info or Web address. If you write your bio offline, create it in plain text in a text editor, not in a word processor. Of course, you'll want to keep this bio reasonably up to date.

For the photo, Amazon asks for a JPEG between 300 and 2500 pixels in both width and height, and no larger than 4MB. Amazon will heavily compress it—so make sure you send a

JPEG of *minimum* compression, highest quality, as a starting point.

As with a book cover image, Amazon will display your photo in a variety of sizes, down to tiny—so it's best to limit the shot to head and shoulders. For the most display area and impact, make your image a square. For high quality, take the photo with a good camera and a long lens. And for the best impression, make the shot casual, friendly, and inviting.

An alternative to using a photo is to have an artist or cartoonist create a portrait of you, even if it's taken from a photo. At a small size, this can often look better and stand out more than a photo would. I currently use a lovely watercolor portrait by the illustrator of one of my children's books. (That is, the *portrait* is lovely, not the subject!)

Author Central also allows you to write a blog on your Author Page. Up to three posts are displayed—your three most recent, with the newest one first. There is no apparent limit to the length of the posts. To access this feature, sign in and click on the Blog tab.

These blogs are carried over from ones that once appeared on authors' book detail pages and on dedicated blog pages through the AmazonConnect program. Even in those days, for most authors, the blogs didn't make much sense if used as intended, because Amazon customers weren't likely to check back for current entries. And that's no more likely now.

My advice, then, is to treat your Author Page blog as not a blog at all, but simply as a way to post three permanent messages to customers. If you never post more than three, they will stay on that page forever, and you can revise content and even titles as needed. (You can't entirely remove a post, but you can make it almost invisible by deleting its content and leaving just a space for the title.)

Subject matter might include

- Extra info and background on your book or books.
- Late-arriving reviews, testimonials, and honors.
- An overview of all your books.
- News of your upcoming books.
- Personal background.
- Special offers and invitations.

You can type your posts directly into Amazon's Web-based editor, but you'll probably find it more convenient to write your text offline and then copy and paste into the editor, adding formatting at that time. As with anything written for online display, you should create it in plain text in a text editor, not in a word processor.

As an option, Amazon's editor allows you to directly edit the "HTML" of your blog post. Be aware, though, that the code is actually XHTML, so you'll have to know the differences. Also, to avoid corruption, the code must be left "compacted"— stripped of the line breaks and indenting normally used to make code easier to follow. If you don't know what you're doing, it's best to leave this alone!

Unlike with other content you submit to Amazon, your blog posts are allowed to include links to other Web sites. There's even a handy button in Amazon's editor to add the links. You can use them to point your readers to extra or enhanced content on your own site or outside blog or anywhere else on the Web.

Amazon's editor provides no way to upload graphics or video—but that doesn't mean you can't insert them, at least if you can work with the code. To place a graphic, add an image tag to the HTML directly and reference an image file on your own Web site or elsewhere online. Keep in mind that an XHTML image tag must include a closing slash. For example, you could add the book cover of *Aiming at Amazon* with this:

```
<img border="1" width="93" height="140"
src="http://www.newselfpublishing.com/books/
AimingAmazon_cover.gif" />
```

With the image in place, you can return if you like to the standard editor to change the alignment.

A side benefit of inserting external graphics is they can be superior to any that Amazon normally displays for your books. Your images can be larger—any reasonable size—and they won't be subject to Amazon's over-compression. You can even keep an sRGB color profile embedded so that color will be more consistent in color-managed browsers like the Safari.

Adding video is trickier, because Amazon disallows the code for embedding. But here's one way around that:

1. Create a page on your own Web site with your video embedded. Include a link back to your Author Page.

2. Using screen capture, create an image of the video player as it displays a select frame of your video. Store the image file on your Web site.

3. Place the image in your blog post by inserting a tag in the HTML.

4. In either the HTML or the standard editor, link the image to the video page on your site.

A simpler though less elegant alternative would be to link the graphic directly to your video on YouTube or another online video service.

One frustrating quirk of Amazon's blog display is that each message is "rolled up." By that I mean Amazon displays only the top two or three inches of each post, with a link below it allowing the customer to view the rest. Clicking the link doesn't take you to a new page but just unfurls the rest of the post, right there on the same page. The problem, of course, is that many customers won't notice the link, and many who *do* won't bother to click it.

The trick, then, is to place content in that two or three inches that will lead customers to notice that link and induce them to click. Two kinds that can do that are a list of testimonials that extends down out of sight, and a large graphic that is obviously cut off.

If you already have a blog outside Amazon and want to put something on your Author Page with no extra effort, Amazon enables you to add an RSS feed. Posts to your outside blog, including graphics, will then automatically appear on your Author Page blog as well.

If you like, you can link to your Author Page from outside Amazon. To get the address, click on the "View your Author Page" button at Author Central, then copy from your browser's address bar. Here, for instance, is how mine looks.

http://www.amazon.com/-/e/B001HD3V8W

To link to it, I would insert this code into the HTML of my outside blog or Web page, all on one line.

```
<a href="http://www.amazon.com/-/e/
B001HD3V8W">Aaron's Author Page</a>
```

Let me stress that you should start from Author Central to collect the address. If you reach your Author Page through any other Amazon link, the address shown in your browser will be much longer, with much in it that isn't needed. If you like, though, you can follow one of those other links, grab your ten-character author code from the address, and replace mine in the address above.

At this writing, Author Central is still in its infancy, so be sure to check it often for new features and opportunities.

Explore More Options

At this point in the chapter, I've discussed all the Amazon features and procedures I consider most useful in promoting and selling your book, plus a few I don't—but there are still a number to consider. Some are moderately helpful, some are nearly useless, and some are downright harmful. You should at least know something about them, so you can decide for yourself whether to pursue them.

If the overall tone of this section seems too negative, remember that learning what you should *not* do is just as important as learning what you *should* do. In fact, some of what I say here may turn out to be more valuable to you than anything else in this book, since it could save you months of work and thousands of dollars.

As you might notice, the approaches I downplay or advise against are ones that "experts" on Amazon marketing often stress as most important. It might help if you understood why this would be.

• Most books on self publishing and book promotion include laundry lists of techniques and resources that sound good but have not been tried by the author.

• The author may have tried the techniques and resources without much success but then, lacking better ideas, recommended them anyway.*

• The author may have tried the techniques and resources and found them helpful, but since then, conditions have changed.

Which brings me to Shepard's Law of Contrarian Marketing. A number of promotional methods on Amazon have

---

* Before devoting time and money to the recommendations of an Amazon "expert," be sure to check the current sales ranks of their earlier books.

worked well enough when first tried. But by the time you hear about one of them from an "expert," years have probably passed, and everybody and their aunt is doing it. You're just one in a huge army, and the method isn't likely to help you much, if any.

Shepard's Law of Contrarian Marketing says, if there's a strategy everyone says is hot, don't bother. You're way too late. Find something that few people have yet caught on to. You want to stand out, not blend in.

For instance, I've talked about the effectiveness of crafting a cover image that's a perfect square, regardless of the shape of the actual book. As far as I know, I was the first book publisher to do this, and the first author to recommend it. But if the idea catches on and everyone does the same, do you think it will still do much good?

No. At that point, you'll be better off with something new—circles, or tilted images, or maybe even the real book cover. Likewise, if everyone starts optimizing and lengthening their subtitles in the way I've developed, you'll be better off with short and pithy ones!

Keep one step ahead in promotion, and you'll keep one step ahead in sales. It's a challenging game, but a fun one—at least for some of us.

Amazon Profile. I've already talked about your Amazon Profile as a convenient access point to many special features. What it's really meant for, though, is to be Amazon's answer to MySpace. Customers can go there to learn more about you or to connect as an "Amazon Friend." You can add personal info and tell Amazon who can see what.

Amazon provides links to your profile from many of your submissions, such as customer reviews and Listmania lists. As I said before, when you're logged in, you can also reach your own profile directly at

www.amazon.com/gp/pdp

When authors and self publishers are told about their Amazon Profile by an "expert" who makes a big deal of it, they often believe that a vital key to success has been revealed. But the truth is that few Amazon customers ever check those profiles or even know they exist. After all, if *you* didn't know about them, why should anyone else?

In fact, an unpublished 2009 survey of Amazon customer viewing patterns showed that one author's profile was visited by less than *one-half percent* the number of customers who looked directly at that author's books. Hardly a source of inspiration! And anyway, at this point, most of the value the profiles might have had has been taken up by Author Pages.

Yes, you should set your profile in order so it doesn't look bad, on the off chance a customer stumbles onto it. But don't expect it to sell a lot of books.

Listmania. This feature allows Amazon customers to list their own recommendations of books in an area of interest. Links to the lists show up mostly on search result pages and toward the bottom of book detail pages.

If you're willing to recommend more than your own book, you can create a list for your book's interest area and place your book first—though of course, for honesty's sake, your comment on it should say that it *is* your book. If the book falls into more than one interest area, you can create a list for each of them. For instance, I placed all my books on reader's theater onto three separate lists: "Reader's Theater," "Children's Plays," and "Teaching Reading Fluency."

For details, click the "Create . . ." link that appears below the list links, or go to

www.amazon.com/listmania

Creating Listmania lists is a good example of a strategy that was effective at first but that has become less and less so—even while it's still heavily promoted by "experts." Though a few authors were successful in promoting their books largely with this strategy, those days are long past. Here's why.

• Amazon now has many more ways to show you related books. So, Listmania list links are no longer displayed as prominently as before, and customers are less likely to feel a need to check them out.

• Very few authors used this strategy at first, so their list links were displayed frequently. With many more authors now competing for fewer display spots, individual list links show up much less often. With a highly specialized topic, you might still see your list linked often when relevant—but with a more general topic, forget it.

• Much of the promotional value of a Listmania list comes not from customers actually reading the list but from their seeing the cover image that Amazon displays with the list link—especially if the image reinforces other appearances of that image to that customer. For a long time, the image Amazon chose to display was simply the first one shown on the list—which on a list meant for promotion would be the author's. Nowadays, though, Amazon chooses the image based on multiple factors, including book popularity—so your list is likely to promote a competitor's book more than your own!

According to the 2009 survey I mentioned earlier, no more than around 1% of customers were likely to visit any given book through a Listmania list link. My advice: Don't spend a lot of effort on 1%.

"So You'd Like to . . . " Guides. These are how-to articles you write that are similar to Listmania lists in featuring your recommendations for books, including your own. Amazon handles them similarly to Listmania lists, and the same general considerations apply. For details, click the "Create . . ." link that appears below guide links, or go to

www.amazon.com/sylt

According to the 2009 survey I've been quoting, "So You'd Like to . . . " Guides accounted for another 1% of customer viewings of a book. Impressed?

Customer Discussions. These allow Amazon customers to comment and ask questions about specific products in a forum setting. The posts appear toward the bottom of a book's detail page. Few books see this feature used heavily, and most get no posts at all—but you might want to check for them now and then on your book's detail page, in case there's a post that needs your response. Oh, and check your Author Page too, since Amazon allows them there as well.

Amapedia. If Amazon's answer to MySpace is the Amazon Profile, its answer to Wikipedia is Amapedia (formerly ProductWikis). Each book detail page has a link near the bottom to take you to the related Amapedia article, or else a link to start one if there isn't any. Details are at

amapedia.amazon.com

Amazon seems to feel it has to jump on the bandwagon for every trendy thing that hits the Web. This is an example of that, with Amazon creating something no one needed or wanted. I don't recommend you bother with it.

Amazon Editorial Reviews. Once upon a time, when Amazon was a happy community of employees in Seattle, the company maintained a large staff that looked over submitted books and wrote reviews of the ones they liked. (Check out the one for Dan Poynter's *Self-Publishing Manual* for a souvenir of those days.)

Now that Amazon is a heartless global juggernaut, it still has a staff to write book reviews, but it's much smaller and focused on promoting big books, especially for publishers paying big bucks for promotion. The chance of a self-published book getting attention is slim—but if you'd like to try, you can send your book to

Amazon.com
Attn: Editorial—Books (Category)
701 Fifth Avenue
Suite 1500
Seattle WA 98104

Replace "Category" with the basic book category that Amazon has assigned to your book.

Amazon Upgrade. This program allows buyers of your printed book to pay a small extra fee to view the entire book online, as well as to bookmark it, highlight passages, and so on. It aims especially at readers who need a book right away, or who want access to a book from anywhere without having to carry it with them. Details are at

www.amazon.com/digitalbooks

Since this program requires being in Search Inside, I have not tried it and can't recommend it. And though I can think of a number of ways it could be put to good use, it doesn't seem to have caught on with Amazon customers. Maybe it's just as well, since the payment that Amazon currently offers publishers is not very exciting.

Small Vendor Co-op Merchandising. This is a program of paid placements for small publishers. Its chief offering is BXGY, or "Buy X, Get Y." BXGY pairs your book with another book for a month, offering the customer an extra discount when buying both. This placement will increase your book's exposure, especially if the other book is a popular one.

The two books are displayed side by side on the detail page for each of them. You'll find them, along with the extra discount offer, in the slot where the "Frequently Bought Together" placements would otherwise go. Amazon currently identifies a paid placement by the name "Best Value"—but whatever it's called, the extra discount tells you it's paid for.

Find details at

www.amazon.com/coop

To understand the nature of this program, it's important to know where it came from. Basically, it's a less expensive version of a program offered to big publishers almost since the beginning of Amazon. But this program was never designed for the publishers' benefit. Instead, it has been a way to make big publishers underwrite Amazon while it sold books at a loss to build market share.

While Amazon may or may not still be selling books at a loss, the publisher co-op program is still a form of forced subsidization of Amazon by big publishers, and now medium-sized ones as well. Amazon has actually threatened all those publishers with discrimination against their books if they did not participate.*

Small Vendor Co-op is less expensive and of course not coercive, but it still continues this fine tradition of Amazon getting more than it gives. The fact is, it's nearly impossible to sell enough books from these promotions to pay for the cost. For almost all self publishers, a paid placement is simply a way to lose hundreds of dollars fast.

---

* See "Amazon Co-op Riles Independent Houses," *Publishers Weekly,* May 31, 2004.

This is even more true now than it used to be. In the past, it was *sometimes* possible to use BXGY to get your book on the Also Bought list of another, recently-published one—a position that could pay off in the long run. But Amazon has since plugged that hole. BXGY sales are apparently no longer counted toward Also Bought listings!

I'll say it again and plainly: In almost every case, BXGY will cost you more money than you can make from it. And if you opt for a pairing with a more popular book at higher cost— as Amazon recommends!—you'll lose even more.

Another weapon in the Small Vendor Co-op arsenal is the Single New Product promotion. For SNP, Amazon designs an email for your new book and sends it to purchasers of similar ones. The email will feature your book but include others that Amazon wants to sell to that audience.

An SNP promotion will currently cost you twice as much as the cheapest BXGY and will probably sell fewer books. While BXGY will appeal to the merely masochistic, SNP caters more to the suicidal.

In case these offerings are not in themselves sufficiently unappealing, Amazon has refused to staff Small Vendor Co-op adequately to handle demand from the hordes of self publishers conned into pulling out their checkbooks. You may have to wait a couple of weeks for a response to email, or it may not come at all—and of course, there's no way to phone. If there's a glitch in your promotion, you may be out your entire fee with no way short of legal action to get restitution or even an explanation.*

---

* This happened to one self publisher whose SNP apparently never went out. He sent several urgent queries over two months and never received a reply. Amazon did not, however, neglect to cash his check—though they neglected that with a different publisher whose promotion *did* go through!

"Instant Amazon bestseller" campaign. This is not an Amazon offering but a popular scheme for gaming the system. In case you haven't heard of it, it's based on a campaign to get a good number of people to buy your book on the same day, pushing the book briefly into Amazon's top 100. Amazon "experts" write about it, laud it, and even charge thousands of dollars to help you do it.

Wake me when it's over.

It's certainly possible to make this happen, but what exactly is the point? Will vaguely calling your book an "Amazon bestseller" really lead to greater sales? Perhaps it would when Amazon was new and when anything "Internet" had a golden aura. But those days are past.

The attempt to create an instant bestseller is most often the desperate effort of a self publisher who has no real idea how to build sales on Amazon. For example, one leading proponent of this method practiced it on one of his own books with great hoopla and, yes, did reach Amazon's top 100—but three years later, that book was not even in Amazon's top 500,000. (To his credit, he told me he's no longer so enamored of the idea.)

Then again, why blame the victim? We might look instead at the high-profile publishing consultants who push such fads so they can collect huge fees for services of questionable value. There are all too many people eager to make fortunes by playing on the hopes and dreams of beginning self publishers. (Hint: Never pay anyone a lot of money to reveal publishing secrets. There are no secrets! Everything you need to know is documented and accessible, and usually cheaply or for free.)

If your book is otherwise effectively marketed, the most you'll accomplish with an instant bestseller campaign will be to shave a few months off the time the book takes to build its momentum on Amazon. That's not likely to pay the campaign's cost. And if the book *isn't* well marketed . . . . Well, you're just throwing away your time and money.

So, forget about "instant bestsellers." Aim to build steady, sustainable, and significant sales, year in and year out—not a flash in the pan.

5
Monitoring Amazon

Watch Availability

Among the most important things about your book you want to keep track of on Amazon is availability—how long Amazon estimates it will take to ship your book, or if it can be ordered at all. This info is displayed on Amazon on your book's detail page and in search results, and it's also included in results at Sales Rank Express.

Unless your book is new or you're making changes to it, the book should *always* have an availability listing like "in stock" or "24 hours" and carry an offer of one-day shipping. That will reflect it's being actually in stock at Amazon, or available from Amazon POD, or available for drop shipping from Ingram or another wholesaler—as are all books printed by Lightning Source—or some combination of these. (In the case of a POD book *not* actually in stock at Amazon, the offer of one-day shipping may include a caveat like "May require an extra 1–2 days." In that case, "one-day shipping" is measured from whenever the book is shipped!)

If your book's availability deteriorates for an unknown reason—which can sometimes happen—you have a problem. But don't panic! First try to figure out the extent of that problem. If you have more than one book, are they all affected, or just the one? If just the one, it could be a temporary glitch—a hiccup in Amazon's system—that could resolve itself within an hour or overnight.

If *all* your books are affected, next check a random sample of books on Amazon. If *no* books are available within 24 hours, you know the problem is in Amazon's computers, and it will be fixed soon enough.

Between these two extremes, keep trying to refine your definition of the problem by figuring out exactly which books are affected. Only yours? Only books from your self publishing company? All books printed only by Lightning Source, or only by Amazon POD? At times like this, it really helps to be in contact with other self publishers—for instance, through a Yahoo group like one of those listed in the appendix. Also, Sales Rank Express can be invaluable in letting you quickly check a number of publishers in turn.

Chances are, the problem isn't even at Amazon, and by pinpointing its range, you can find the most likely source. For instance, if most books printed only by Lightning Source suddenly dropped from "24 hours" to "1 to 2 weeks," it would suggest a glitch at Ingram, which could itself suddenly fail to show the books as available for drop shipping.

Even for problems originating at Amazon, most are transient, or else big enough that they get fixed without your attention. But if you do need to intervene personally, send a message through the General Questions contact form, possibly citing the Book Catalog Department as the intended recipient. Be as specific as possible and *identify each of your affected books by ASIN (ISBN-10)*.

If you don't get a satisfactory response, or the problem isn't fixed, *keep after them*. You might also try to enlist your POD service to push from the other side, though there's no guarantee they'll be any more effective.

Actual stocking of your book by Amazon—or its failure to stock—can be an indicator of the book's progress. If your book is selling well, Amazon is likely to order it in quantity and stock it in one of its own warehouses. This is instead of relying on drop shipping by Ingram—as Amazon does for most books printed by Lightning, due to low sales—or even on printing by Amazon POD.

But if Amazon always *says* a POD book is "in stock" or "24 hours," how can you tell if Amazon *really* stocks it? As I mentioned, for a book *not* really in stock, you might see a statement like, "May require an extra 1–2 days." Also, for a book *really* in stock, Amazon will say exactly how many hours and minutes you have left to order for delivery on a certain date. And when Amazon has *real* stock, but five or fewer copies, it may state that number.

While actual stocking status is usually a good sign of how well your book is doing, there are a number of circumstances in which it fails to tell the whole story and so may be misleading. These include

• Amazon may be ordering the book for stock but is temporarily out.

• Amazon may be ordering the book for stock but in low enough quantities that it's *always* out. (This is the long-standing condition of my book *The Business of Writing for Children*.)

• Amazon may have copies in stock because it can't sell the one or two it ordered!

• Amazon has stopped or started ordering for stock because it's adjusting its inventory level.

So, while it's nice to see that Amazon is really stocking your book, don't get hung up on it if it isn't.

Watch Sales Ranks

When you aim at Amazon, you need a certain amount of patience. Though a well-written and well-published book should start selling almost at once, it will generally take about a year to reach its full potential. (Yes, you read that right. A year!)

That's because, as the book begins to succeed, its success feeds more success. Amazon's sales mechanisms and dynamics gradually lift a winner toward the top. It just takes a while.

But what can you look at to follow your book's progress and gauge that success? The most direct indicator, of course, would be sales figures. Amazon itself won't give you those—but if you published through CreateSpace or BookSurge, *all* your reported sales would be through Amazon.com. And even if you worked with a different self publishing company or directly with Lightning Source, Amazon.com would typically contribute 75% to 90% of sales.

What sales figures won't tell you, though, is your book's *relative* position on Amazon—relative to other books, including direct competitors. It also won't provide *timely* feedback. For those, you need to look at your book's Amazon sales rank.

I've already discussed the meaning of sales ranks when I talked about researching the market for your book, and I also mentioned there are tools that can help you follow them. One of these, again, is my own free Sales Rank Express, at

www.salesrankexpress.com

Sales Rank Express lets you search for books by any combination of author, publisher, title, and ISBN, listing up to 4,000 results. The sales ranks shown are up-to-the-second, exactly reflecting what you would find on Amazon itself. S.R.E.

also lets you quickly check the sales ranks of up to ten competitors by using the "Get Pairings" button that appears next to your book in results. (I'll talk more about pairings.) It even offers a Web Widget that can display your book's current sales rank on your Web site or blog.

As the premier sales rank *checker,* Sales Rank Express is unsurpassed for closely following sales ranks. For long-term analysis, though, you may want to supplement it with a sales rank *tracker.* This kind of tool watches a title's sales ranks for you and gives you averages and charts for various periods.

One drawback of trackers is that most don't collect ranks hourly, so they miss the height of the jumps that signify sales. *This makes your sales ranks look lower than they should.* In fact, some trackers collect ranks only once daily, and only at night, when a book's rank may be skewed higher or lower.

Among the trackers, my current favorite is TitleZ—still in Beta and still free after many years. Here are the addresses for that one and several others you might try.

> **www.titlez.com**
> **www.ranktracer.com**
> **www.rankforest.com**
> **www.booksandwriters.com**

You might also try SalesRankWatcher, a free Windows program from Paradoxal Press.

> **www.paradoxalpress.com**

Your book acquires a sales rank as soon as it starts selling—and if it has no sales rank, that means it hasn't sold! An exception is some erotica and other "adult" books. Amazon may withhold sales ranks from these to prevent their appearance in some search results and bestseller lists.

As I explained earlier, *all* sales ranks are updated all together each hour. But that doesn't mean you'll see a particular sale reflected at the next hourly update. My tests found a typical time lag at Amazon of around two to three hours between a sale and a corresponding jump in rank. It can be longer too—for instance, if Ingram is slow to confirm a drop ship order, or if Amazon's sales rank computing system stalls for a while.

If you're like many authors and self publishers, you're likely to check your sales ranks a good deal more often than you need to. If so, try not to be spooked by natural variations. Sales and ranks of particular books often vary by season, by day of the week, and by time of day.

For instance, my book *The Business of Writing for Children* tends to sell best on weekdays during working hours, and falls off at night, on weekends, and during the summer. In other words, it does best when teachers and librarians get their high-speed Internet access at work, and when stay-at-home mothers have their kids in school! And every year, Morris Rosenthal has to remind me that *most* books sink in the ranks in the back-to-school months of August and January as students load up on required texts.

Besides these predictable variations, all sales have a natural ebb and flow that defies logical analysis. You may have seen this in grocery stores, where seemingly everyone in the store will suddenly flock to the cash registers. I first noticed it myself in a former career as a wandering peddler, selling bamboo flutes on the street. I would get a rush of sales, then nothing, a rush of sales, then nothing, in a fairly regular cycle of about half an hour.

So, don't get hung up on every little rise or fall in your sales rank. It's going to happen. But if you see an unexpected change that *stays* that way for a while—or if you see a rise when you expected a fall—or vice versa—then you might want to look for a cause. This might be a change or addition on Amazon, or something outside it, like a review or recommendation.

You can gauge the nature of the variation also by keeping an eye on the sales ranks of your book's chief competitors, as Sales Rank Express makes easy with its "Get Pairings" button. If the *relative* positions of your book's sales rank and its competitors' stay roughly the same, then you can figure that any shifts are due to general variations on Amazon as a whole or for books like yours. But if your book rises and stays higher in regard to the others, or if it sinks and stays lower, then that's another sign something has changed for your book alone.

Finally, keep in mind that *all* sales ranks for *all* books will tend to fall over time—with increasingly volatile jumps—as Amazon expands its catalog with more and more books that attract buyers. It's Amazon's own brand of inflation! But the good news is, as Amazon's market share keeps growing, each sales rank comes to represent higher sales.

With a book that has moderate sales, it's not hard to "ride" the sales rank and get a close count of total Amazon sales by noting each jump. But when doing this, some authors make the mistake of then scurrying over to their POD service and looking for those same sales in that day's sales report. Not finding them, they conclude they're being cheated.

Jumps in sales rank indicate sales of your book by Amazon *and nothing more*. They do *not* indicate sales by your POD service, and they will *not* match up to your sales reports.

There's a variety of reasons for this. In one simple case, let's say a book is printed only by Lightning Source, and neither Amazon nor Ingram actually has it in stock. When a customer buys the book, Amazon will place an order with Ingram for drop shipping, and Ingram will in turn order a copy from

Lightning. All of that is on Day 1—the day the publisher sees the jump and says, "Aha!"

As of mid-2009, Lightning takes only about four hours to print a book and deliver it to Ingram—but for the sake of our example, let's say the order comes late in the day. Because it doesn't go out till next morning, Lightning doesn't record the sale till then. That's Day 2. But recorded sales don't show up on Lightning's computers till after an overnight refresh. So, we're already on Day 3, two days after Amazon's sale.

A self publisher working directly with Lightning will be able to see the sale on Day 3. But if they're instead working with a self publishing company that handles those dealings—well, who knows how long it will take the record of that sale to migrate to the company's reporting system.

The relationship between Amazon's sale and yours becomes even more distant if either Ingram or Amazon is actually stocking the book. Typically, Amazon will try to maintain several weeks of stock for any book that's selling well. That means it might be placing small orders to replace whatever copies it sells. But it might wait a day or two to do that, or a couple of weeks—or it might not do it at all, if it decides to reduce inventory.

Meanwhile, the particular copy that Amazon sells was likely ordered and sold to Amazon weeks *before*. Which means the publisher should be looking in the sales report of the *previous month,* or even earlier! And the same might be true if the book is stocked by Ingram.

This example was for a book printed only by Lightning Source, but the same things can happen with Amazon POD. The sale will be recorded only when the book is sold to *Amazon,* not to its *customer*. And that sale to Amazon could come later, or it could come well before—because Amazon may keep a stock of books even if printed by Amazon POD!

Besides general sales ranks, Amazon provides category sales ranks for books appearing on any of Amazon's bestseller lists. As I mentioned before, Amazon maintains such a list for each book category, however specialized, showing its top 100 sellers. You can access the lists from the toolbar at the top of Amazon book pages, or go to

www.amazon.com/bestsellers

If your book places on any of these lists, up to three categories and ranks are displayed on your book's detail page, right below the general sales rank. The rank is updated every hour, along with the bestseller list itself.

Watch Search Results

Another important indicator of progress on Amazon is your book's search results placement—where on the list the book shows up from a search. Though Amazon now has other ways for customers to find books, direct search was one of the original and may still be how customers most often begin sessions.

If you researched your markets as I suggested, you already know the phrases used most often to find your kind of book. So, plug these into Amazon's search function and see how your book fares. Try searches both in all departments at once (the default) and in books only. Note that book search results are unlimited but all-department results are restricted to a few pages—so in those, your book may not show up at all.

The default sort order for book search results is by "Relevance." To figure this, Amazon takes into account a number of factors, which may include:
- Sales rank.
- Order, placement, and frequency of search words in the book's title and description.
- Availability.
- Assigned categories.
- Analysis of Search Inside text.
- Appearances in Listmania lists.
- Tags applied by customers.
- Purchases with similar books.
- How often a book is clicked on in search results.
- How often the book is purchased from a search.

As some of these factors improve for a book, it gradually moves up in results—and as it moves higher, sales rank and click numbers tend to improve. So, the book keeps rising until and unless it hits a ceiling of books that Amazon finds "more relevant."

Of course, the higher your book rises, the better. A customer may not go beyond the first page of results, or even past the first listing. Still, any position on the first couple of pages is pretty good.

Though search results on specific phrases can change a bit from day to day, major changes occur only a couple of times a week. That's how often Amazon "rebuilds the catalog"—in other words, recompiles all its book and sales data and re-sorts its various lists. These rebuilds occur overnight, generally on Monday and Thursday mornings.

Because of Amazon's constant tinkering with its systems, it's common for a rebuild to fail completely. In that case, the rebuild is attempted again the next day, and so on till it manages to reach the end.

But even when it completes, a rebuild can be wonky, and this shows up nowhere better than in search results. It's not unusual for a book to suddenly drop down several pages in the results, or even to disappear entirely. Don't panic! Chances are that the situation will correct itself in the next rebuild. Or if your book doesn't spring back from a poor position, it will almost surely rise again by the same forces that lifted it in the first place.

Watch Pairings

Originally, Amazon's great strength as a bookseller was the searchability of its vast offerings. Since then, that advantage has been surpassed by another: Amazon's ever-growing ability to pair similar books for recommendations to customers. With this, Amazon has managed to emulate within its gigantic operation the kind of hand-selling found mostly in small bookshops. According to the 2009 study I cited in the last chapter, on Amazon customers' viewing patterns, 45% of one popular book's detail page views came from Amazon recommendations—almost half!*

Because Amazon doesn't directly refer to the products of this underlying technology, I call them *pairings*—though you might also call them "Also Boughts," on the strength of one well-known use. As that name suggests, they're based mostly on a pattern of a number of customers buying the same two books, including any linked formats or editions of either one.†

The two books do not need to be purchased at the same time. Instead, Amazon apparently combs and collates the entire buying history of all its customers—and does it twice a week, with each catalog rebuild. Pretty impressive!

There's no apparent limit to the number of pairings for each book. But Amazon makes sure each pairing is relevant

---

* Figures for other referrer types included 19% for external links to Amazon from around the Web, 25% for links from Amazon search results, and only 8% for links from all Amazon Community features put together—those features that Amazon marketing "experts" usually stress. Counting only Amazon's internal links and ignoring external ones, the figures were 55% for recommendations, 31% for search, and 10% for Community.

† For simplicity, I talk here only about pairings between books—but actually, books can be paired with anything sold on Amazon. This is most often seen between books and movies.

by setting a minimum threshold of joint purchases. It also discards pairings that might occur just because one book is especially popular.

Each of a book's pairings is ranked against the others in order of significance, based mostly on the number of customers making the dual purchases. The ranking may also take into account such factors as book categories, tags applied by customers, and analysis of Search Inside text. Books unavailable on Amazon may be omitted.

The pairings calculated by Amazon are then drawn on for several types of recommendations. The oldest and best known of these are the "Frequently Bought Together" placements (formerly called "Better Together") and the "Also Bought" listing, both found on a book's detail page.

Frequently Bought Together is Amazon's prime recommendation of an additional one or two books to buy. The first recommended book is simply Amazon's top pairing for that title. The second one may be the #2 pairing, or for reasons known only to Amazon, one from farther down the list. Sometimes the Frequently Bought Together position is taken over by a paid placement—but in that case, it gets a name like "Best Value" and shows an offer of additional discount.

Right below Frequently Bought Together is the Also Bought listing, appearing under a heading like "Customers Who Bought This Item Also Bought." The listing is currently shown as a row of books, with clickable arrows at the ends for displaying more rows. The number of books displayed at a time is adjusted to the width of the window in the customer's browser—so, the farther the book to the right, the fewer customers will see it in the first row.

This listing comprises *all* of the book's pairings, and it's the only place they can all be seen. The pairings are mostly shown from left to right in order of rank, though the top pairing is shifted down the list so it won't so obviously duplicate the Frequently Bought Together.

Appearance in Also Bought listings and Frequently Bought Together placements can greatly help a book. Many Amazon customers simply keep clicking from the Also Bought listing on one book's detail page to the listing on another to find the most popular books on a subject. This can reveal books the customer would never find with a search.

Amazon may use pairings to assail customers with recommendations on almost any part of the site. The first recommendations you see when you visit Amazon's home page while signed in are likely to come from these pairings. And so are Amazon's top "exit offers"—the recommendations you see when Amazon confirms you've placed a book in your shopping cart. In each case, Amazon will omit books you've already bought with the account you're signed into.

Yet another form of recommendations is email promotions. Amazon may send such messages to recommend books paired to ones you've bought.

Taking a broad look, here's how all these features work in the advancement of your book: If your book is succeeding, then customers who buy popular books on its subject will also buy yours. As that happens, you should see your book appear on the Also Bought listings of those other books and slowly start rising in position. As the pairings become stronger, your book may appear in the first rows of those listings and also begin to be recommended elsewhere on Amazon to individual customers.

At that point, your book could be doing very well indeed. But as I suggested earlier, it can easily take a year before this gradual rise is complete. So, take a deep breath, sit tight, and enjoy the very . . . slow . . . ride.

Though you can follow the progress of your pairings by visiting Amazon, Sales Rank Express offers a method that is generally more convenient and that avoids some of Amazon's minor on-site manipulations. It's done by "chaining," and it's actually one of S.R.E.'s most powerful features.

First call up your book in S.R.E. results and press the "Get Pairings" button you see to the right. This displays the top ten pairings for your book, in order of significance. If you check on Amazon—which you can do just by clicking your book's title at the top of S.R.E.'s page—you should see that the #1 pairing shown by S.R.E. is the first book shown by Amazon for Frequently Bought Together, unless a paid placement has taken its place.

Back at the pairings on S.R.E., click the "Get Pairings" button for each of the ten books listed. This will quickly show you the top ten pairings for each of *those* books. What you're looking for is *your* book and its position on *those* lists. The more lists your book appears on, and the higher it has risen on each, the greater your marketing strength on Amazon.

As an example, let's take a look at my book *Stories on Stage,* a collection of scripts for reader's theater. After searching on S.R.E. and getting a listing, I click the "Get Pairings" button to see the top ten. Right from that page, I can already see that my book is noted as the "Top Pairing" for three books, including my own two other reader's theater books.

For the other books listed there, I click each "Get Pairings" button in turn and look for *Stories on Stage* among that other book's pairings. In this way I find that my book appears twice at the #2 position, once at #4, once at #6, once at #7, and once at #8, with only one no-show among any book's top ten. That's not bad!

While you're checking those other books' pairings, keep an eye out for new competitors rising from below! If a book on these lists is butting up against yours or passing it, this may signal a need to refine or amplify your marketing—and maybe to learn from the other's success.

At times, S.R.E.'s "Get Pairings" feature can help not only to gauge the progress of a book and its competitors but also to alert you to missteps and machinations of Amazon itself. If you see a sudden radical shift in positions, or if S.R.E.'s pairings are completely different from the ones you see on Amazon— you can bet that something's up! *

---

* In the summer of 2006, Amazon made changes in its formulas for pairing that seemed to favor books sold to Amazon on better terms, as well as books with higher cover prices. This discrimination—possibly from nothing more than a programming error—grew gradually stronger but was then removed at the beginning of 2007. Sales Rank Express, by making it easy to check pairing positions of particular titles, proved extremely helpful in documenting the rise and fall of the effects. Some of this info was presented to Amazon and may even have helped encourage the problem's resolution.

Watch Rivalries

With sales ranks fluctuating so wildly, and with pairings changing position so glacially, Amazon's info on your book's *rivalries* is perhaps the most helpful marketing feedback it will give you.

Like *pairings, rivalries* is my name for something Amazon deals with but never quite names. This info, appearing only once your book has attained a respectable level of sales, is found mainly on book detail pages under a heading like, "What Do Customers Ultimately Buy After Viewing This Item?" While Also Bought listings tell you which books are bought *together*, Ultimately Buy listings look at which books are bought *instead*. (That's even though both tend to show the same books!)

To be more exact, Ultimately Buy listings tell you the few books that customers most often buy during a shopping session in which they view your book's detail page—that is, if they buy any book at all—along with the percentage of such purchases each book can claim. For any book that appears on Amazon in linked formats or editions, their sales are counted together. A book not available for sale by Amazon itself may be omitted.*

OK, that's a bit complex, so let's look at a concrete example. Here's a simplified rendering of the Ultimately Buy listing for my wife, Anne's, book *Smart Soapmaking* on a pleasant day in August 2008.

> 85% buy *Smart Soapmaking*
> 4% buy *The Soapmaker's Companion*
> 4% buy *Making Natural Liquid Soaps*
> 3% buy *Soapmaking for Fun and Profit*

---

* Here again, as with pairings, I'm simplifying by talking only about books, though other kinds of items can be rivals.

What this listing means is, of the Amazon customers who've been visiting the *Smart Soapmaking* detail page, 85% of the ones who bought *any* book bought this one. *The Soapmaker's Companion* and *Making Natural Liquid Soaps* were each bought by another 4%, while 3% bought *Soapmaking for Fun and Profit.*

You may notice that the figures don't add up to 100%. That's because the list shows only the four top rivals, while some of the customers in question will have bought a book that didn't make the list. From another angle, you might expect the figures to sometimes add up to *more* than 100%, since some of those customers will have bought more than one book. But the sums apparently never do go higher—so there's probably some kind of limiter in the formula.

Since many customers may view your book's detail page then not buy *any* book, these figures do *not* tell you the page's *sell-through*—the percentage of customers who buy your book after viewing the page.* What the figures *do* indicate is the marketing effectiveness of what's on that page in comparison to what's on the detail pages of similar books. (Or at least, they *mostly* indicate that. The figures can be skewed if Amazon is visited by a number of customers already meaning to buy a certain book.)

Basically, there are two things you hope to see in your book's Ultimately Buy listing. First, you want your book to be listed at the top, with the highest percentage—as in our example above. If you don't get the bulk of purchases by customers viewing your own book's detail page, then your marketing or

---

* The 2009 independent study I mentioned earlier in this chapter also made a tentative calculation of sell-through in relation to a book's Ultimately Buy figure on its own page. Sell-through was estimated to be on average around five times lower.

your book may be lacking. And if your book isn't even on the list . . . . Well, you have a long, hard road ahead of you.

Second, you want your book's percentage to be as high as possible! Here's a rough guide to the desirability of different percentage ranges.

> 90% and up—Amazing!
> 80% and up—Excellent
> 70% and up—Very good
> 60% and up—Good
> 50% and up—OK
> Under 50%—Help!

Third—though of course we would never wish poor sales on our competitors—it's always nice to see that your book's percentage is a whole lot higher than theirs.

Besides checking the Ultimately Buy listing on your *own* book's detail page, you may want to check it on the pages of its rivals. Each book has an advantage on its own page, so you need to look at the others for a fair comparison. For each book you compare, what you hope to see is, first, that your book is listed on its rival's page at all, and second, that each of the two pages shows your book with a higher percentage than its rival has on the other.

Confusing? I expect it is! So, let's go back to *Smart Soapmaking*. Here again is the listing on that book's detail page.

> 85% buy *Smart Soapmaking*
> 4% buy *The Soapmaker's Companion*
> 4% buy *Making Natural Liquid Soaps*
> 3% buy *Soapmaking for Fun and Profit*

Clearly, the figures look good for Anne's book—in fact, they're the best I've seen for any book I've published! While her book is at 85%, *The Soapmaker's Companion,* her closest rival, is at only 4%. But how does that rival do on its own detail page? Here are the figures:

48% buy *The Soapmaker's Companion*
26% buy *Smart Soapmaking*
10% buy *The Everything Soapmaking Book*
9% buy *Making Natural Liquid Soaps*

As you can see, the 85% shown for *Smart Soapmaking* on its own page is higher than the 48% shown for *The Soapmaker's Companion* on *that* book's page. And the 26% shown for *Smart Soapmaking* on its rival's page is higher than the 4% shown for its rival on the page for *Smart Soapmaking*. Just what I wanted!

If you see this pattern for your book, what it tells you is, given an equal number of visitors to each book's detail page, your book will probably outsell its rival. Not surprisingly, Amazon seems to respond to such higher figures by moving a book up in search results to drive more customers to it. (At the time of these examples, *Smart Soapmaking* was #1 in Amazon's search results for both "soapmaking" and "soap making.")

The Ultimately Buy listings are not only an analytical tool but also a predictive one in regard to Amazon's pairings. As I said, Also Bought and Ultimately Buy listings tend to show the same books—but not without significant differences. Aside from the ways the listings are calculated, Also Bought listings use data that is much more long-term. Ultimately Buy listings, focused on more recent sales, tend to show where Amazon's pairings are *going.*

What this means is, if Amazon shows your book in another book's Ultimately Buy listing, you can expect your book to become one of that other book's top pairings, if it isn't already. And if your book places *highest* on that Ultimately Buy listing among all that other book's rivals, your book is likely to become its *top* pairing.

And in fact, that is what happened to *Smart Soapmaking*. Already at the time of this example, it was the #3 pairing for *The Soapmaker's Companion*. Within one year, it had become the #1 pairing and the first book shown as Frequently Bought Together. To reach this position, Anne's book had to overcome the long sales history of its rival together with most other books it was paired with—not to mention the previous #1 being another soapmaking book by the same author! Still, the extreme pattern of percentages in our example made Anne's capture of this position a pretty safe bet.

The key to improving your book's position in rivalries is to strengthen your book's detail page—in other words, to go back through *this* book and see how to apply more of the tips I've given, or how to apply them better. As your book's detail page becomes stronger, you should clearly see that reflected in the rise of your book's figures and the fall of its rivals'— sometimes starting within days.

By the way, if you're waiting for me to tell you how much more conveniently you can check rivalries on Sales Rank Express, I'll have to disappoint you. This info is not shared by Amazon for outside use—at least not yet—so S.R.E. cannot include it. But of course, you can use the links in S.R.E. results to quickly visit pages on which you want to check Ultimately Buy listings.

Watch Customer Reviews

Customer reviews can make or break a book, so you'll certainly want to keep an eye on them. Of course, you can do that on the book's detail page. You can also do it in Sales Rank Express, which makes it easy to track additions by giving you the review total, the date of the latest review, and a link to Amazon's page for all the reviews, newest first.

With all the abuse by authors and publishers of the Customer Reviews feature, you may well become a victim of it yourself. For instance, a competitor might post a review of your book that is unfairly negative or clearly aims to steal sales. Sadly, it has also become common for a regular reader to trash a book on impulse, assigning a single star without considering how much harm this might do to a sincere and hardworking author—or perhaps even fully intending such harm.

If your book suffers abuse, you can complain to Amazon's Community Help and ask for a review's removal. Use the Features and Services contact form, or send email to

Community-Help@amazon.com

Be sure to specify the title, author, and date of the review, along with your book's title and ASIN (ISBN-10). Customer comments on reviews can be reported the same way. Someone at Amazon will then take a look and see whether the review or comment violates company guidelines.

Those guidelines, which are posted in Amazon Help, list certain no-no's you might specifically point out to Community Help. These include
- Profanity, obscenity, or spiteful remarks.
- A focus solely on the author instead of the book.
- Spoilers.

- Time-sensitive statements.
- More than one Web site address.
- A phone number or postal address.
- Comments on other customer reviews.
- Solicitations for "Helpful" votes.
- Mentions of price or availability (which can change).
- Corrections to the listing (which should go through the Catalog Update Form).
- Any type of promotion, advertising, or solicitation.

You can cite other things as well, such as the fact that the reviewer is a direct competitor, or that some remarks are libelous or defamatory. One argument I've found effective is to point out that the reviewer did not actually read most of the book. Often a reviewer will say as much, either directly or indirectly, as in stating they "returned the book" or "stopped reading." Or they may give themselves away with a blatantly false statement about the book's content.

If your message reaches someone at Amazon who agrees with you, the customer review or comment might be removed within days or even hours. Other times, just the bit that's objectionable might be snipped out—for instance, a quoted price. (If one of a review's comments is removed but others remain, the missing one will be replaced by a notice of the deletion.)

If you don't get what you want, you can send the request again. That way, you might reach someone more cooperative. Nowadays, though, with Amazon outsourcing this branch of customer service overseas, the likelihood of getting someone cooperative is very high.

In fact, many authors and self publishers are taking advantage of this to get rid of any review at all that they don't like. This is just as unethical as manufacturing positive ones, and undermines Amazon just as badly. If someone reads your book carefully, finds reasonable cause not to like it, and expresses their views in a civil fashion, their opinion should be respected.

But isn't there anything you can responsibly do about such reviews? The best thing, again, is simply to encourage the writing of customer reviews by more people who have read and liked the book.

If a negative review has nothing to warrant removal, you can consider posting a comment yourself to counteract it. But avoid coming off as whiny or defensive. You should limit yourself to such aims as correcting facts, clearing up misunderstandings, pointing out oversights, and offering helpful suggestions. Keep your tone friendly, or at least keep it even, and do *not* insult the reviewer or argue against their opinion. Of course, if you have evidence that the review is phony but you can't get Amazon to remove it, then the gloves are off!

Sometimes a negative review can be a gift in disguise. Consider whether your book might benefit from changes to meet the reviewer's criticisms. Often the comments most helpful to us come from those who don't like our books. Such a reviewer might be doing you a favor by telling you things that other readers think but don't say. And sometimes a surprisingly small change can fix the problem.

There's always an urge to hash things out with a negative reviewer. As I said, sometimes you can find contact info in a reviewer's linked Amazon Profile, or enough personal info in the review and/or the profile that you can identify the reviewer and find contact info on the Web.

If the reviewer was reasonable and you just want to discuss a point or two, there's nothing wrong with making contact. But if the reviewer was grossly unfair, irrational, or abusive, I suggest you forget it. Rather than helping the situation, you're more likely to inspire the reviewer to further acts of hostility.

With such reviewers, it's best to deal with their review quietly and behind the scenes by going directly to Amazon.

Which brings me to another piece of advice: *Don't invite negative customer reviews by giving them yourself.* However unfair it may seem, it's basically unwise for any author or publisher to post negative reviews of other books on Amazon, regardless of how sincerely and strongly you feel they deserve it. We're all much too vulnerable to get involved with that. You never know when you're going to anger someone who will decide to take it out on you and your books, and possibly with more skill and vigor than you can handle.

An occasional negative review of your book among positive ones should not seriously hurt it. In fact, it may prevent customers from suspecting fraud even when there's none! It may also help turn away other potential negative reviewers who would share the same objections. And a medley of strongly positive and strongly negative reviews may even help sales by generating controversy.

And if your customer reviews are *mostly* negative? Well, take it as a learning experience. Rewrite your book, start a new one, or just move on!

While standing watch over your customer reviews, don't neglect your efforts to attract new ones. You may at some point think you have enough, and customers may think so too. But Amazon promotes your book based partly on the number of reviews it has garnered and partly on their currency—so you can always use more.

Watch Tags

You can watch your book's tags on its detail page, and also on Sales Rank Express. S.R.E. conveniently counts not *tags* but *taggings*—the number of tags applied, multiplied by the number of customers applying each one—a handy "score" not shown on Amazon. S.R.E. also gives you a link to an Amazon page with all the tags for your book.

The sheer number of taggings is a good indicator of progress on Amazon, but to explore how this is helping your book's marketing, you'll need to look farther. Most of Amazon's use of tags is invisibly incorporated in search results, recommendations to customers, and such—but here and there it surfaces in a way that at least gives some sense of how your book is faring.

Here's how to see one of these. From your book's detail page or its page of tags, click on tags with phrases that customers might use to search for your book. Each link will bring you to a page with more books and other items receiving that tag, displayed in rows similar to the kind Amazon uses for its Also Bought listings. Items that have received that tag most often or most recently will be in the first row—and that's where you want to see your book. The farther left it's placed, the more likely that Amazon is recommending your book to customers seeking books of that kind.

For example, if I go to the detail page for my wife, Anne's, book *Smart Soapmaking,* I can click on the tag that I believe is the book's most important search phrase, "soapmaking." The link takes me to a page showing thirty-seven products tagged with this phrase. Anne's book, which Amazon says has been tagged with it eighteen times, is in the first row, at far left. Perfect!

Amazon's use of tags for your book can also be seen in a feature labeled, "Looking for . . . Products? Other customers suggested these items." This list currently appears on a book's detail page just above the book's tags—but it appears *only* when the page is reached from a link in search results, and then *only* when the search phrase has also been used as a tag. What the list really shows is the few other items that have received the same tag the most times, and what Amazon gives as the number of customers suggesting the item is really the number of customers who applied that tag.

To see how your book is benefiting from this, enter one of your book's important tags as a search phrase, then click on any one of the top results—other than your own book—to get to the book's detail page. What you hope to see is your book among the few items that Amazon says customers have suggested.

For example, if I wanted to check *Smart Soapmaking,* I'd search on "soapmaking." Choosing one of the other top results, I might click on *The Soapmaker's Companion.* Sure enough, there in first place is the recommendation for Anne's book, which Amazon says was suggested by eighteen customers—the same number, you remember, that Amazon said had applied that tag.

Watch Other Content

As your book gains exposure and builds interest, customers will create more and more content around it—not only reviews and taggings, but also Listmania lists, "So You'd Like to . . . " guides, and forum discussions. Multiplied by the various views offered by Amazon, this means your book can show up on literally thousands of pages. You can get a sense of your book's penetration with a site-specific Google search, such as this one for *Aiming at Amazon.*

site:www.amazon.com "Aiming at Amazon"

Be sure to include the quote marks!

6
Pointing to Amazon

Channel Your Sales

As I've explained, the better your book sells on Amazon, the more Amazon promotes it with improved placements, recommendations, and so on—so the better it sells. It's a "virtuous cycle." So, when aiming at Amazon, you don't just want your book to sell more copies, you want it to sell as many as possible *on Amazon.*

This means, whenever and wherever people are looking for your book, you should encourage them to go to Amazon to buy it. If you instead sell books directly from your Web site, you undercut your position on Amazon. If you direct people to their local bookstore, your book suffers on Amazon. If you send people to BN.com . . . . Well, you get the picture.

If you have a popular Web site or blog, that's one good way to point visitors to Amazon. Include links or buttons to take the visitor directly to your book's detail page there. Do you also have an email newsletter in which you promote your books? In my own such email promotions, I typically provide one link to the book's page on my site, and one to its detail page on Amazon.

A link to your book on Amazon might also go in the "signature" at the bottom of your email messages, especially if you don't have your own Web site to promote. This signature can be especially effective if you participate in email discussion groups on the book's subject.

Your links might or might not generate loads of sales on Amazon, but even a few can have a significant effect on your book. This is especially true when you first launch the book and it has no sales record. Just a few sales can "prime the pump," bringing your book far enough up in Amazon search results so that other customers start noticing it. Later, in lean times, those few sales may keep your book from slipping out of sight.

Some self publishers balk at sending customers to Amazon, because they assume they can make significantly more per copy by taking orders directly. This would not be so if you were working directly with Lightning Source and setting a short discount—but even in other cases, it's most often beside the point. Sales on Amazon generate *more* sales, in a way that your direct sales cannot. When Amazon takes the business, you make more profit.

But what if you have other, more profitable "information products" to sell as a follow-up to your book? Doesn't it pay to sell direct to the customer so you get the lead? That may certainly be true—but if you go that route, at least understand the price you pay in book sales.

And if your heart—like mine—is in the books themselves, keep aiming at Amazon.

Earn Commissions

Since you're sending visitors to Amazon to buy your book, be sure to sign up for Amazon.com's affiliate program, called Amazon Associates. (Don't confuse this with Amazon Advantage!) This program will give you a percentage of what your visitor spends when they get there, either on your book or on other items sold by Amazon or third-party vendors. If your Web site or blog is popular, that can add up to hundreds of dollars per quarter.

You can join from anywhere in the world. Payment is by gift certificate, by check, or within the U.S., by direct bank deposit. Find details at

affiliate-program.amazon.com

Or if you want an address easier to remember,

www.amazon.com/associates

Amazon provides its associates with a wide variety of links, forms, and widgets for placement on your Web site. But these Amazon constructions play a number of tricks and may not land the visitor directly on your book's detail page. You may prefer, then, to construct your own links and buttons, even if it means sometimes earning a lower commission. In the next section, I'll show you how to do some of this, and you can see more of my code by visiting my Web site and viewing the HTML source in your browser.

If you're a programmer and want to work Associates links into your own Web-based application, you can sign up for the Associates program Product Advertising API—formerly part of Amazon Web Services under various other names—which provides direct access to Amazon marketing data. (This is the service powering Sales Rank Express.) Sign in to Associates and look for the link to this program, or go directly to

**affiliate-program.amazon.com/gp/
advertising/api/detail/main.html**

Be aware, though, that support for this service has declined. So, any bugs you find—and there are many—are not likely to be corrected.

Tame Your Links

Amazon Web addresses tend to confuse people, and you often see them presented improperly—even in published books, and occasionally even in correspondence from Amazon!

Most authors and self publishers simply navigate to their book's detail page on Amazon.com and copy the address from the browser. For this book, *Aiming at Amazon,* that might give you something like this:

> http://www.amazon.com/gp/product/093849743X/
> ref=sr_11_1/103-8344352-0086236?ie=UTF8

Yes, you *could* use it like that. But what you should understand is that only part of that address is actually needed to get to the page. The entire last half is simply Amazon talking to itself about your visit. If you include everything you see, you only make it intimidating—and clicking on it in email might not even work, if the address breaks between two lines.

Here's the functional part of the address:

> http://www.amazon.com/gp/product/093849743X

Better, yes?

This is not really standard Web addressing, though, so I'll tell you what it does: When your browser accesses Amazon at this address, the site passes your request to a program referred to as "gp."

> http://www.amazon.com/**gp**/product/093849743X

The request is for a detail page to be assembled from Amazon's info on a specific "product."

http://www.amazon.com/gp/**product**/093849743X

And the product is *Aiming at Amazon,* identified by the number "093849743X"—the book's ASIN. (As I explained before, that's the "Amazon Standard Identification Number," which for most books is identical to the ISBN in its older, ten-digit version.)

http://www.amazon.com/gp/product/**093849743X**

If you were putting the Amazon address directly in your browser, you could also leave off the "http://" prefix, which would be filled in by the browser itself.

www.amazon.com/gp/product/093849743X

But never leave off the prefix in email, because it tells email programs that the address should be displayed as a link. Without the prefix, the reader of your email may not find the address clickable.

Here's a sample of another, newer form of Web address you might collect from Amazon.

http://www.amazon.com/Aiming-Amazon-
Publishing-Successful-Amazon-com/
dp/093849743X/sr=1-26/qid=1157218790/
ref=sr_1_26/002-1785957-5192848?
ie=UTF8&s=books

This address accesses the "dp" program in place of "gp." Again, the second half is just Amazon chatter, and we can leave it off.

http://www.amazon.com/Aiming-Amazon-
Publishing-Successful-Amazon-com/
dp/093849743X

But there's something new here as well: The address includes keywords from the book's title.

http://www.amazon.com/**Aiming-Amazon-Publishing-Successful-Amazon-com**/dp/093849743X

These keywords aren't really there for addressing at all—you could remove them or replace them with any words you like and still reach the page. They're only there for the benefit of Google and other search engines, as a way to improve the position of Amazon pages in search results. At least until Google catches on!

Stripping away the keywords too, you get a wonderfully compact address for a book.

http://www.amazon.com/dp/093849743X

What if you want to add your Amazon Associates ID for a commission on sales? It would look like this:

http://www.amazon.com/dp/093849743X/ref=nosim?tag=simpleproduction

In this address, "simpleproduction" is my Associates ID, while "ref=nosim" is a "switch" that makes Amazon take you directly to the book's detail page—instead of to a "Similarities Page," which would show similar titles as well. Like all other Web addresses, this one must be entered as a continuous string, with no spaces or line breaks. (In other words, don't break any of these addresses into multiple lines as I show them here—I've done that only for presenting them in this book.)

Here's an older form of address that also incorporates your Associates ID, this time while accessing the "obidos" program.

> http://www.amazon.com/exec/obidos/ASIN/
> 093849743X/simpleproduction/ref=nosim

"Obidos" forms of address like this have been phased out of internal use by Amazon—but for external links, they'll still be supported for the foreseeable future, and it's good to have them as a backup. You never know when a newer form of address might stop working properly!*

If you like, you can shorten this address a bit by abbreviating "exec/obidos" as "o."

> http://www.amazon.com/o/ASIN/093849743X/
> simpleproduction/ref=nosim

For email, any of the addresses shown above with Associates ID are long enough that some software might break them into two lines before they reach their recipient. If that happens, only the first line may be clickable. But the link should still go to your book's detail page—you'll just lose your commission.

To avoid even that, you might try enclosing the address in angle brackets. Most email programs will then properly handle the address whether it falls on one line or many.

> <http://www.amazon.com/o/ASIN/093849743X/
> simpleproduction/ref=nosim>

---

* Obidos is the single, unified software program that originally ran *all* of Amazon.com. It has now been replaced by a collection of specialized programs, and the requests sent to it are redirected.

Alongside such addresses for specific, individual books, there are addresses for starting searches from offsite. Here's one that displays all books by that illustrious author Aaron Shepard. (Remember not to include any spaces or line breaks in this.)

http://www.amazon.com/gp/search?
index=books&field-author=Aaron+Shepard

As you can see, this is another "gp" address, but one that requests a "search" instead of a "product." In this case, the search is for "author," but you can substitute "publisher," "keywords," "subject," or "isbn." (All of these terms, including "isbn," must be entirely lower case.)

A "keywords" search can be especially useful to find multiple versions of a single book if Amazon hasn't linked them together. To identify the book, it's generally enough to include two or three words from the title plus the author's last name.

The "isbn" search works with either thirteen-digit ISBNs or the older, ten-digit ones. Either variety can also be used in a "keywords" search—and in fact, that kind will sometimes locate a book when an "isbn" search won't.

If you like, you can abbreviate "gp/search" in that address as "s."

http://www.amazon.com/s?
index=books&field-author=Aaron+Shepard

You can add your Associates ID here too. It would look like this:

http://www.amazon.com/gp/search?
tag=simpleproduction&index=books
&field-author=Aaron+Shepard

There's also an older, "obidos" form of search address that does much the same—though, again, it may or may not keep working for as long as the newer form.

> http://www.amazon.com/exec/obidos/external-search?
> tag=simpleproduction&mode=books
> &field-author=Aaron+Shepard

You may be wondering at the odd punctuation in some of these addresses—question marks, equal signs, plus signs, and ampersands. The question mark tells the accessed program to look at the *variables* that follow it—text or values you're telling the program to plug into its operation. (Sometimes you see a slash placed before the question mark, but that's redundant and not really good form.)

The variables themselves, translated into plain English, each take the form "this is that"—"author is Aaron Shepard," or "search index is books," or "Associates ID is simpleproduction." The equal sign (=) is the *is*, while the plus sign (+) stands in for a space between words, since you're not allowed to include a space itself in the address. The ampersand (&) is just an *and* that separates the variables.

The order of the variables is completely optional. For example, in the first search address above, they could as easily have been reversed like this:

> http://www.amazon.com/gp/search?
> field-author=Aaron+Shepard&index=books

If you leave the most "variable" variable at the end, though, you'll have an easier time if you ever have to modify numerous addresses by find-and-replace.

I've written the search addresses above as they'd appear in your browser or as they'd be placed in an email message. But when coding one into a standard HTML link on your Web site, the most reliable form is to replace each ampersand (&) with the ampersand entity (&). For example, in an HTML link, the first search address above would look something like this:

```
<a href="http://www.amazon.com/gp/search?
index=books&amp;field-author=Aaron+Shepard">
Aaron at Amazon</a>
```

Since Amazon's preferred address forms do change over time, you might check my Publishing Page for the online version of this discussion, which I'll try to keep up to date. (In that version, the addresses shown are clickable links, so you can also easily check where they take you.) If you're an Amazon Associate, you should also be able to get help in the Associates forums.

Of course, you'll want to test any form of address thoroughly before deploying it widely through your Web site or broadcasting it by email. When testing it, though, be aware that Amazon will not pay commission on any order you place through an Associate link of your own, even if from a different Amazon account. They do have ways of knowing!

7
Updating for Amazon

Refine Your Book

As you follow the progress of your book, and observe reactions to it, and live with it longer yourself, you're likely to feel that some things could have been done better.

Perhaps you didn't think of an obvious phrase that someone might search on. Or something in the book wasn't explained quite clearly. Or your main character is called Oliver in one scene and Olivia in the rest. Or your face on the back cover is just a bit too dark a shade of green. Or it really might matter that your page numbers change to Roman numerals halfway through.

One of the best things about print on demand, especially for beginners in publishing, is that nothing is carved in stone. While you might not have found it worthwhile to reprint 5,000 copies to fix a misspelling of your spouse's name, the correction is no more than a slightly costly inconvenience with POD.

I've talked about how crucial your book's subtitle is to the book's success on Amazon, and about how to replace a shorter subtitle with a longer one. The same methods can be used later as well, to refine or entirely replace your subtitle. If you care about subtitles as much as I do, you're likely to keep thinking of ways to improve the one for a nonfiction book long after publication. In fact, it has become a standing joke between my wife, Anne, and me that I'm "changing subtitles again."

Ideas for changes can come from discovering new search phrases that customers might use for books like yours, or from an attempt to broaden or better define your market, or even from changes in the way Amazon searches.

For instance, for *The Business of Writing for Children,* one segment of the subtitle used to be "Writing and Publishing Children's Books." This included all the words in this subject's most popular search term, "writing children's books." But while first writing *Aiming at Amazon,* I noticed that Amazon seemed to have started assigning a greater Relevance score to titles with all three words together *as a phrase.* So, I changed that part of my subtitle to "Writing Children's Books and Publishing Them"—and this did in fact seem to help.

Doesn't it get expensive to keep changing subtitles? Not really. Because, as I realized long ago, *the subtitle listed online does not have to match the subtitle in the book.* And in fact, I often don't even print more than a short form of the subtitle in the book, giving me an even freer hand in changing the long version. As for the cover, I usually put *no* part of the subtitle there, where it would be most difficult to change and where it would make departures most noticeable.

I remember when the penny dropped for me about subtitles. I had purchased a book on Amazon called *Gandhi: A Photo Biography.* When I wanted to mention it on one of my Web sites, I checked the book to make sure that Amazon had listed the subtitle correctly.

There was no subtitle. Anywhere.

It was then that I understood that subtitles can be purely a marketing tool. The one in your book and the one online can be completely different entities. Since then, I've never bothered changing the subtitle in a book unless I'm revising it for other reasons.

As you might imagine, I'm just as finicky and fickle about my cover images as about my subtitles. As I learn to design and produce better images, I replace my old ones on Amazon. The boost in sales can be substantial—in one case, they about doubled!

Refresh Your Content

With nonfiction, people want up-to-date information, and if your book doesn't provide it, they'll try to find one that can. The last thing you want is a customer review calling your book outdated. So, if you want to keep selling it at the same level, you have to keep it reasonably current.

We've talked about minor improvements in your book after publication, which are common and accepted with print on demand. But updating raises other issues entirely. In fact, with the way print on demand makes updates so easy, it challenges the whole concept of "edition."

In traditional book publishing, updating a book is a major effort and expense. A new edition can generally be managed only every few years, if at all. When it *is* accomplished, it's marked by new identifiers for the book, including a new ISBN for each format. In other words, a new edition is pretty much considered a new book.

But with print on demand, you could even find yourself updating a book every few months, especially if you were handling production yourself and using a word processor, with its built-in flexibility. A book of resource listings, for instance, could be frequently refreshed.

Would you then send each update to your POD service as a new edition—a new book requiring a new ISBN? Probably not, because that would make the whole updating process ponderous, more expensive, and possibly not worthwhile. You would also risk complications with your Amazon listings, which could lead to reduced sales and customer confusion.

But what if you waited several years and then overhauled the book, the way traditional publishers do? Would you make it a new edition then? Where would you draw the line on whether that was needed?

I'm not going to provide a definitive answer for you, because I don't have one. The traditional book world relies on the sanctity of the ISBN. Issuing a major update under an old ISBN would be considered a major publishing offense.

On the other hand, print on demand and online bookselling are forming a whole new world, and the old identifiers simply don't function the same way. In traditional publishing, for instance, a new edition brings renewed interest in the book and a rise in sales. On Amazon too, a new edition might encourage long-term sales—but in the short term, confusion related to your book's listing can cause sales to drop, as well as mislead customers into buying the outdated version of your book.

Amazon has gotten better at managing the transition between old and new editions, but it still has a ways to go. So, how can a self publisher be blamed for deciding to "update in place"—publish a major revision without changing the ISBN?*

Still, updating in place may not always provide the greatest advantage, even to a POD publisher. Here are some reasons you might still favor a new edition.

• You plan to make a big promotional push. That's easier to do with a brand new release, because anything new is more likely to be seen as meriting attention.

---

* Because even discussing "updating in place" is a radical departure in a book on self publishing, I know there are some who will consider this approach flat out unethical. So, let me state clearly that this is not an ethical issue at all. The standard rules of ISBNs are publishing conventions and nothing more. Whether or not it's wise or professional to flout such conventions—and I'll leave that for you to decide—there is nothing immoral or illegal about it. In fact, the practice benefits Amazon's customers, who are otherwise likely to buy the wrong book.

• You've rewritten or added so much that customers really are getting a different book. A new edition can lessen the confusion of customers expecting what the book *used* to be.

• You need the book to appear recent. This might influence not only Amazon's customers, but also Amazon itself. Amazon sometimes appears to favor new books in its promotions, giving them significantly greater visibility.

With a new edition, you can show customers it *is* new by adding an identifier to the end of your subtitle—"2nd Edition" or the like, perhaps in parentheses. (Remember to fit it all within the 200-character limit for title and subtitle combined.) Amazon will of course list your new pub date in the details for the new edition, but it can also show there an edition specifier you submit via the Catalog Update Form.

For an update in place, by contrast, Amazon currently gives you *no* way to show currency. If you try a subtitle addition—for instance, something like "2009 Update"—Amazon will likely reject it, stating that a new edition requires a new ISBN. The same may happen if you try to change the pub date or edition specifier—and besides, either of those changes could lead to confusion and, if misinterpreted, leave you open to charges of dishonesty. So, at this point, you'll just have to accept that customers won't know from the book's detail page that your book is up to date.

Let's say for now you do decide to issue a new edition, with new ISBN and all. There are two ways that this new edition might get set up on Amazon. In the first way, the new edition is *linked* to the old. I've already talked about linking formats and editions in my discussion of adding content to your book's detail page. Amazon will probably link the editions for you automatically, based on your editions having the same title.

The advantage of this linking is that the new edition retains all the customer reviews and ratings of the old. The *dis*advantage is that only one edition of the book will show up at a time in search results, Also Bought listings, and such—and that might not be the edition you want. For instance, Amazon has tended to show the edition that has the lowest-priced copy on sale, new or used—and for a while at least, that often means the older edition.

In other cases, a new edition might *not* be automatically linked by Amazon to an older one. This happens most commonly if the new edition has a slightly different title. For instance, the *2006 Writer's Market* and the *2005 Writer's Market* were not linked originally—though Amazon seems to have later taken care of this.

The advantage of the editions *not* being linked is there's no danger of Amazon hiding the new edition behind the old, either intentionally or through confusion. The disadvantage is, in terms of marketing, your book is back to square one. It has to acquire new customer reviews and slowly rise in search results and other listings which, as I said, can take a year. Meanwhile, it's still competing with used copies of the old edition, which is listed separately.

At this point, it's probably best to make sure your editions are linked. If you see that they're not, you can request linking through the Books Content Update Form by entering both of the ISBNs when submitting new content (or resubmitting old), or by going through Amazon's General Questions contact form with a message for the Book Catalog Department. But be sure that's what you really want. Once the editions are linked, you probably can't get that reversed.

In any case, whether they're linked or not, you may be able to mitigate the competition from an older edition. To prevent it from showing up as often in search results, you can simply *remove the subtitle*—by submitting a title correction that omits it.

Some issues arise whether you're issuing a new edition *or* updating in place—though the solutions may not be the same in each case. For starters, how do you keep from angering buyers of the earlier version who learn that your revision has appeared soon after their purchase—or maybe even before?

You might consider halting sales of the old version before the new one comes out. Two months should be long enough to let stock sell out at Amazon, to let returned copies sell again, and then to leave what previous buyers might consider a reasonable interval. (If old copies linger too long, you might consider buying up some yourself.) But I must caution you against halting sales before the new version is ready to go. With one version of *Aiming at Amazon,* for instance, I lost four additional months of sales when I discovered I couldn't complete it when planned.

Even with a halt in sales, you may still get complaints from disgruntled readers who feel cheated. Though it's not really your fault or responsibility, it might be worthwhile to send them a PDF file of the updated book, or even a printed copy.

8
Globalizing with Amazon

Aim at Amazons

The market for English-language books is growing world-wide, and Amazon is helping it. Books printed by Lightning Source will show up on Amazon in the U.S., Canada, the U.K., France, Germany, and Japan. Amazon POD's author services are at this writing limited to U.S. sales—but its publisher services have already spread to the U.K. and Germany, with author services sure to follow.

By recycling and tweaking many of the materials and methods you use for Amazon.com—Amazon's U.S. site—you can build sales in other countries into a significant supplement to your book's income. With moderate effort, those sales can add 10% or more to the total.

Optimize for Amazons

While even very American books can sell abroad, it's worth your while to think how you can increase your book's international appeal. For an example, take my wife, Anne's, book *Smart Soapmaking*. To help it sell better abroad, we made the little extra effort to include measurements in metric units as well as in traditional ones. And where necessary, we included British equivalent terms in parentheses throughout the text.

For the back of the book, Anne had compiled a list of American suppliers she liked to buy from. To supplement it, we used Yahoo Groups to contact soapmakers in Canada, the U.K., and Australia for recommendations of suppliers in those countries as well. We also sent copies of the text to soapmakers in the U.K. group so we could make sure the book made sense in that part of the world.

In these contacts, what probably impressed Anne most was how *glad* these soapmakers were to have an American publisher take them into account. Almost all the soapmaking books they could buy came from the U.S., and *all* of those books ignored anyone and anything in other countries.

Now, when those soapmakers recommend a book to beginners, whose do you think it will be?

Similar steps could be taken if you're outside the U.S. but wanting to target its book buyers. Make sure your book can be understood and used as well by Americans as by those in your own country. There's no sense confusing readers in what can easily be your biggest market.

Access Amazons

Here are the Web addresses for Amazon's sites outside the U.S.

> **www.amazon.ca** (Canada)
> **www.amazon.co.uk** (U.K.)
> **www.amazon.fr** (France)
> **www.amazon.de** (Germany)
> **www.amazon.co.jp** (Japan)*

Amazon also owns a Chinese site called Amazon Joyo (formerly Joyo.com). But that one is not as tied in to the Amazon system and does not carry books from U.S. POD services, so I'll ignore it here. You can see it, though, at

> **www.amazon.cn**

Some Amazon functions, like correcting data, require you to sign in to your account. You'll find that any account you have on Amazon in the U.S., Canada, the U.K., France, or Germany, will carry over to all the rest—so just sign in with your usual email address and password. At this writing, though, Amazon in Japan makes you create a separate account just for that site. (But you can sign up with the same email address and password as for the others.)

Where accounts are shared among sites, purchase histories still are not. If a feature requires you to make a purchase before contributing, it has to be *from that site.*

---

* An alternative address for Amazon in Japan is www.amazon.jp. But it is not the official address and doesn't work in all contexts.

Amazon, of course, shows you a sign-in/sign-up page whenever it's called for. But if you need to go to one directly, just use one of the following addresses.

www.amazon.ca/gp/sign-in.html (Canada)
www.amazon.co.uk/gp/sign-in.html (U.K.)
www.amazon.fr/gp/sign-in.html (France)
www.amazon.de/gp/sign-in.html (Germany)
www.amazon.co.jp/gp/sign-in.html (Japan)

Here are terms you may need to recognize when signing up, signing in, or accessing your account. From left to right, the languages are English, French, German, and Japanese. Some "translations" are actually equivalents instead, but they're the ones used by Amazon.

E-mail address • Adresse e-mail • E-Mail-Adresse • Ｅメールアドレス
New customer • Nouveau client • Neuer Kunde • 初めて利用し
Password • Mot de passe • Passwort • パスワードを
Name • Nom • Name • 氏名
Retype • Confirmer • Nochmal eingeben • もう一度入力して
Birthday • Anniversaire • Geburtstag • 誕生日
Your Account • Votre compte • Mein Konto • アカウントサービス

Amazon has been making basic functions more and more consistent among its sites, so figuring out how to deal with them usually isn't too hard. And don't worry, I'll give you specific Web addresses for functions on each site. But by far the simplest way to deal with them is through Sales Rank Express. There you'll find the links and buttons to let you do a number of jobs quickly for each country.

www.salesrankexpress.com

Amazon's publishers guides too may help you find resources, even if you don't really read the language and have to poke around. Here are the addresses. (Amazon in France doesn't have one.)

www.amazon.ca/publishers (Canada)
www.amazon.co.uk/publishers (U.K.)
www.amazon.de/verleger (Germany)
www.amazon.co.jp/publishers (Japan)

Like Amazon.com, Amazon's other sites maintain one online contact form for General Questions and another for Features and Services (though the specific topics covered by the latter form vary from site to site). You can access any of these forms through the "Contact" links on Sales Rank Express, clicking on each country's tab to see the links for it.

To reach the General Questions contact form for any country while on its site, you can use a button on any Help page. You can also reach the forms with these direct addresses.

www.amazon.ca/gp/help/contact-us/
general-questions.html (Canada)
www.amazon.co.uk/gp/help/contact-us/
general-questions.html (U.K.)
www.amazon.fr/gp/help/contact-us/
general-questions.html (France)
www.amazon.de/gp/help/contact-us/
general-questions.html (Germany)
www.amazon.co.jp/gp/help/contact-us/
general-questions.html (Japan)

For the Features and Services contact forms, you can use these.

**www.amazon.ca/gp/help/contact-us/
features-and-services.html** (Canada)
**www.amazon.co.uk/gp/help/contact-us/
features-and-services.html** (U.K.)
**www.amazon.fr/gp/help/contact-us/
features-and-services.html** (France)
**www.amazon.de/gp/help/contact-us/
features-and-services.html** (Germany)
**www.amazon.co.jp/gp/help/contact-us/
features-and-services.html** (Japan)

As with any Web address shown in this book on two lines, make sure you enter each of these in your browser in one continuous string, with no line break or space.

Non-English sites will also have a special contact form for English speakers. Access the site's main Help page, then look for a link for English help. Contact buttons on those English pages will lead you to the English form—even if the button isn't in English! Here's what to look for:

Help • Aide • Hilfe • ヘルプ
Contact Us • Contactez-nous • Kontaktieren Sie uns •
カスタマーサービスに連絡

You can also use these direct addresses.

**www.amazon.fr/gp/help/contact-us/
english-speaking-customer.html** (France)
**www.amazon.de/gp/help/contact-us/
english-speaking-customer.html**
(Germany)
**www.amazon.co.jp/gp/help/contact-us/
english-speaking-customer.html** (Japan)

You'll notice that a number of the addresses I'm giving are simply the U.S. address with a change of domain—the part before the first slash—to identify the country. This is often a good way to search for equivalent Web forms or info among the different sites.

Obviously, when working with these sites, you may need help with more terms than I'm able to translate for you here. Web forms are fairly consistent among Amazon sites, so you may be able to figure them out just by comparing them. But if not, you can get at least a rough idea of what they're saying with a translation program or service such as Google Translate.

translate.google.com

Market on Amazons

Amazon.com—Amazon's U.S. site—is not only the biggest of Amazon's sites in terms of sales, it's also the prototype for all the others. Amazon has been working hard to standardize software and features across all its sites. Still, less successful features may never get to those other sites, and even those that are successful may take quite some time. For example, at this writing, Author Pages are found only on Amazon in the U.S. So, you may have to check a site to see whether a particular opportunity is available for marketing.

For listings, those sites get their book info and content from a variety of sources. Amazon in the U.K. relies for basic info mostly on Nielsen BookData, a listing service that compiles data from publishers and POD services, including Lightning Source UK. But for availability of books not in stock, Amazon looks at Gardners and Bertrams|THE, the two largest British book wholesalers. Both of these offer all books printed by Lightning UK—but they don't drop ship for Amazon as Ingram does in the U.S. So, you never get 24-hour availability in the U.K. unless Amazon stocks the book.

Amazon in France, Germany, and Japan also gets its info for books in English primarily from Nielsen BookData. But for these sites, Amazon may order the book from either the U.K. or the U.S., depending on where it can get the best deal—and nowadays, with the weak dollar and lower printing costs, that's most often in the U.S. As for Amazon in Canada, it can go toward either the U.S. or the U.K. for both info and buying, but it gives priority to the U.S. and to Ingram.*

---

* Apparently, books sent to Amazon in France, Germany, and Japan from the U.S. are actually ordered for those sites by Amazon's U.S. staff. For Amazon in Canada, U.S. staff has been ordering *all* its books, since Amazon

Of course, the need to import books from the U.S. or the U.K. can greatly add to posted availability times. It generally also means a higher price charged by Amazon, through either a reduced discount or a surcharge—though this might be masked by the currency conversion.

POD books are spread among the Amazon sites also by Marketplace sellers from the U.S. and the U.K. who order from wholesalers and ship internationally. Because of differences in currency and suppliers, this sometimes means Marketplace sellers can substantially undercut Amazon's prices, as U.S. sellers often do on Amazon in the U.K. This also means that a book printed by Lightning Source will show up on all these sites even if you try to limit distribution.

Overall, the easiest way to check your book listings on Amazon's many sites is through Sales Rank Express. Just click on the tab for the country you want. (If your book is in English but the Amazon site isn't, be sure to select "Imported" in S.R.E.'s search options.) In the results, S.R.E. will even translate many terms into English for you.

Of course, you can also use the sites' own search forms. On the non-English sites, you can find books in English when searching in all departments at once (the default) or when searching just in "English books." You will *not* find them when searching in books in general, or in books in that country's language. Note that your book's ISBN is the same anywhere in the world, so you can search for that on any site, in either its thirteen-digit or its ten-digit form.

Here are some terms you may need when searching.

---

has had *no* physical presence in Canada, handling all Canadian warehousing and fulfillment by outsourcing. But this looks like it may change, with Amazon's 2008 acquisition of AbeBooks, a Canadian company.

Books • Livres en français • Bücher • 和書
(English books) • Livres en anglais • Englische Bücher • 洋書
Relevance • Pertinence • Beste Ergebnisse • キーワードに関連する商品
Bestselling • Meilleures ventes • Topseller • 売れている順番
Price: Low to High • Prix : par ordre croissant • Preis: aufsteigend •
価格の安い順番
Price: High to Low • Prix : par ordre décroissant • Preis: absteigend •
価格の高い順番
Avg. Customer Review • Note moyenne des commentaires •
Kundenbewertung • おすすめ度
Publication Date • Date de parution • Erscheinungsdatum •
出版年月が新しい順番

You can also use the following addresses to go directly to your book. Just substitute your book's ASIN (ISBN-10) for the one shown here for *Aiming at Amazon*. (Since your book's ISBN is the same worldwide, so is its ASIN.)

www.amazon.ca/dp/093849743X (Canada)
www.amazon.co.uk/dp/093849743X (U.K.)
www.amazon.fr/dp/093849743X (France)
www.amazon.de/dp/093849743X (Germany)
www.amazon.co.jp/dp/093849743X (Japan)

If you're already on your book's detail page on Amazon.com or any of the other sites, here's a shortcut to get to it on the others: Change just the domain—the part of the Web address before the first slash—in your browser's address bar and hit Return (Enter). For instance, if you were viewing your book on Amazon.com and wanted to see it at Amazon in Japan, you would just change "com" to "co.jp".

Here are some terms that will help you check out your listings. First, terms for bindings:

Hardcover • Relié • Gebundene Ausgabe • ハードカバー
Library Binding • Belle reliure • Bibliothekseinband • 図書館
Paperback • Broché • Taschenbuch • ペーパーバック
Mass Market Paperback • Poche • Klebebindung • マスマーケット
Print on Demand • Print on Demand • BOD • オンデマンド

Terms for contributor types:

Author • Auteur • Autor • 著
Illustrator • Illustrations • Illustrator • イラスト
Editor • Sous la direction de • Herausgeber • 編集
Translator • Traduction • Übersetzer • 翻訳
Preface/Foreword • Préface • Vorwort • はしがき
Introduction • Introduction • Einleitung • 序論

Terms for availability:

In Stock • En stock • Auf Lager • 在庫あり
Months • Mois • Monaten • 月
Weeks • Semaines • Wochen • 週
Days • Jours • Tagen • 日
Hours • Heures (h) • Stunden • 時間
Minutes • Minutes (min) • Minuten • 分
Not yet published • À paraître • Noch nicht erschienen • 近日発売
Temporarily out of stock • Temporairement en rupture de stock •
Derzeit nicht auf Lager • 一時的に在庫切れです

Note that, if your book title is in English, all the sites will
list it as is, even if that's the only English on the page.

As with errors on Amazon.com, errors on these sites are
likely to originate upstream, so check there first. If you want to
make a change just on the Amazon site, you can reach that
site's equivalent of the Catalog Update Form with the "Fix

Data" button in S.R.E. results, or with the link near the bottom of your book detail page on the site itself. Look for

Update product info • Compléter ou améliorer les informations • Produktinformationen aktualisieren • 更新する

Or use these direct addresses, swapping your book's ASIN for the one here for *Aiming at Amazon.*

www.amazon.ca/gp/gfix/welcome.html?
ASIN=093849743X (Canada)
www.amazon.co.uk/gp/gfix/welcome.html?
ASIN=093849743X (U.K.)
www.amazon.fr/gp/gfix/welcome.html?
ASIN=093849743X (France)
www.amazon.de/gp/gfix/welcome.html?
ASIN=093849743X (Germany)
www.amazon.co.jp/gp/gfix/welcome.html?
ASIN=093849743X (Japan)

Some of the terms given above to help you read listings will help also when handling the correction forms, and so will the following. (Dashes are shown when Amazon's form in that language omits a field.)

Title • Titre • Titel • タイトル
Author • Auteur • Verfasser • 著者
Binding • Reliure • Einband • 版型
Publication Date • Date de parution • Erscheinungsdatum • 出版日
Publisher • Éditeur • Verlag • 出版社名
Number of Pages • Nombre de pages • Seitenzahl • ページ数
Edition • Édition • Auflage • エディション
Volume • — • — • 巻
Format • Format • Format • —

Language • Langue • Sprache • 言語
References • Références • Quellenangaben • リファレンス
Preview • Prévisualisez • Vorschau • 更新をプレビューする
Submit • Valider • Absenden • 更新を送信する
Edit • Modifier • Berichtigen • 更新を編集する

When asked to supply the address of an authoritative Web page, you have an added option with these countries: You can cite your book's detail page on Amazon.com, assuming you've gotten the info there just as you want it.

Content you submit for your book's detail page is generally not shared among Amazon sites, so you'll have to submit to them individually. All except France have an equivalent to the Books Catalog Update Form on Amazon.com. To find the forms, use the links at Sales Rank Express—just click the country tab to view the one you want. Or go directly with one of these addresses.

> **www.amazon.ca/gp/content-form?**
> **product=books** (Canada)
> **www.amazon.co.uk/gp/content-form?**
> **product=books** (U.K.)
> **www.amazon.de/gp/content-form?**
> **product=books** (Germany)
> **www.amazon.co.jp/gp/content-form?**
> **product=books** (Japan)

These shortcut addresses still work too.

> **www.amazon.ca/add-content-books** (Canada)
> **www.amazon.co.uk/add-content-books** (U.K.)
> **www.amazon.de/verleger-texte** (Germany)
> **www.amazon.co.jp/add-content-books** (Japan)

Note that all those content forms are for books in the language of that country. (The Canadian form is also for books in French.) For Amazon in Germany and Japan, there are also special forms for books in English—though the forms themselves aren't in that language. (Go figure.) Both of those forms accept English content for posting without translation. Here are the addresses.

**www.amazon.de/gp/content-form?
product=books-intl-de** (Germany)
**www.amazon.co.jp/gp/content-form?
product=english-books** (Japan)

or

www.amazon.de/publisher-texte (Germany)
**www.amazon.co.jp/
add-content-english-books** (Japan)

Here are terms you'll need for content forms, this time without French.

Publisher • Verlag • 出版社
Contact person • Kontaktname • 氏名
Contact e-mail • Kontakt-E-Mail • Eメールアドレス
Mailing address • Postadresse • 連絡先住所
City/Town • Stadt • 区市町村
State/Province/County • 都道府県
Country • Land • 国
ZIP/Postal code • Postleitzahl • 郵便番号
Phone • Telefonnummer • 電話番号
Description • Kurzbeschreibung • 出版社/著者からの内容紹介
Publisher's comments • Verlag über das Buch • 出版社からのコメント
Author comments • Der Autor über das Buch • 著者からのコメント

Author bio(s) • Über den Autor • 著者について
Table of contents • Inhaltsverzeichnis • 目次
Inside-flap copy • Klappentext • カバーの折り返しにある文章
Source • Quelle • ソース
Review • Rezension • レビュー
Excerpt/First chapter • Auszug aus • 抜粋
Continue • Weiter • 次に進む
Submit • Senden • 送信する
Edit • Bearbeiten • 編集

You may wonder why Amazon in France has no book content form, as well as no publishers guide. At this writing, that site relies on an outside agency for its book data, and imports its English-language content from other Amazon sites—though you can still correct the basics.

Amazon shares book cover images among all its sites—so if your image has made it onto Amazon.com or any one of the other sites, it will already be on them all. But if it hasn't gotten there yet and your book is printed by Lightning UK, the image will arrive through Nielsen.

Tags on non-English sites—*mots-clés* in French, タグ in Japanese—present a special opportunity. Instead of just submitting the same tags as for the U.S, Canada, and the U.K., you can submit them in the site's native language. That way, a customer searching in all departments on a phrase in their own language may find your book too. Such a customer might well be able to read a book in English yet never think of searching for one.

Google Translate is a good starting point for help with translations. Again, you can find that at

translate.google.com

Another good resource is Wikipedia, which has parallel, linked articles in a variety of languages.

www.wikipedia.com

Look for links that say "Français" (French), "Deutsch" (German), and "日本語" (Japanese).

But wherever you start, be careful to tag with phrases that might actually be used by a native speaker. A literal translation often won't work. So, make sure any phrase you're considering is used on Web sites in that language or in titles of similar books. (In Web search results, don't confuse Japanese with Chinese, which has mostly the same characters but may use them in a different way.)

Some phrases won't need translation at all. Names of people, places, and organizations, plus many modern or technical terms, may migrate in English form directly into another language. Again, look around to see how or whether a phrase is used.

Monitor Amazons

As with Amazon.com, Sales Rank Express is the most efficient tool for keeping tabs on your books on Amazon's five other sites. It's especially helpful where you don't understand the site's language, as it does much of the work of translation.

Sales ranks are figured separately for Amazon in each country. On non-English sites, a book in English will have *two* sales ranks—one for books in general, and one for books in English. It's generally the English books rank you'll see on the site—and in Sales Rank Express—though Amazon may show the other rank too.

All sites have Frequently Bought Together placements, Also Bought listings, and Ultimately Buy listings. You should have no trouble recognizing them, regardless of language.

For help with abusive customer reviews on Amazon in the U.K., you can write to

reviews-help@www.amazon.co.uk

Point to Amazons

The Web has no borders. If you're linking to Amazon.com through your Web site or email, it makes sense to link to Amazon in other countries too. Just as for Amazon in the U.S., every sale encourages Amazon to lift your book higher on the site where it's made, attracting more sales.

And if you're linking to those sites, you might also want to sign up for the affiliate program of one or more of them, even though the revenue will be much less than for the U.S. (Each site pays only on its own sales.) The addresses are

> **associates.amazon.ca** (Canada)
> **affiliate-program.amazon.co.uk** (U.K.)
> **partenaires.amazon.fr** (France)
> **partnernet.amazon.de** (Germany)
> **affiliate.amazon.co.jp** (Japan)

Or these, if they're simpler to remember.

> **www.amazon.ca/associates** (Canada)
> **www.amazon.co.uk/associates** (U.K.)
> **www.amazon.fr/partenaires** (France)
> **www.amazon.de/partner** (Germany)
> **www.amazon.co.jp/associates** (Japan)

For most Amazon sites, you can be paid by gift certificate, by check, or within your own country, by direct bank deposit. Checks are sent only when you're owed a certain minimum amount. Gift certificates can be a nice alternative, as they let you avoid the payment minimum and also the hassle of handling checks in foreign currency. You can use gift certificates to buy things you can't get in your own country, or to order your own books for testing or as gifts for foreign friends.

To build links to Amazon outside the U.S., use any of the forms of link I discussed for Amazon.com and replace the "www.amazon.com" with the other site's domain. For example, here's the simplest address for *Aiming at Amazon* in the U.K.

http://www.amazon.co.uk/dp/093849743X

If you're including an Associates ID, remember that you need a different one for each country. Also, for a non-English site, a search for books in English requires a change in the "index"—or "mode," as it's called in "obidos" addresses. Here is the address for a "gp" search for my books on Amazon in Japan. (For an "obidos" search, you would use this same index name for the mode.)

http://www.amazon.co.jp/gp/search?
index=books-jp-intl-us&field-author=Aaron+Shepard

For the index or mode name used in another country, replace the "jp" with "fr" for Amazon in France, or "de" for Amazon in Germany. Or for any of these countries, use the older but still recognized mode name "books-us," like so.

http://www.amazon.co.jp/gp/search?
index=books-us&field-author=Aaron+Shepard

Note that the "us" in these index names is a nickname to signify all books in English, whether or not from the U.S.

Appendix

Where to Get Help

I'm always glad to receive feedback on my books, but I'm afraid I can't offer consulting, mentoring, or other private guidance, paid or unpaid. (Strangely enough, I actually make my living from publishing, not from talking about it!) For personal help, please try the following:

For help when working with self publishing companies—POD author services—see the online forums operated by those companies, or join the Yahoo group Print-on-Demand.

groups.yahoo.com/group/Print-On-Demand

For help when working with POD *publisher* services such as Lightning Source, join the Yahoo group pod_publishers. (That's where I hang out, myself.)

groups.yahoo.com/group/pod_publishers

To find consultants who can help you work with Lightning, see "Other Publishing Resources" on my Publishing Page.

For help when pursuing traditional self publishing—which may now include POD and sales through online booksellers but doesn't focus on them—join the Yahoo group Self-Publishing.

groups.yahoo.com/group/Self-Publishing

Amazon Etiquette*

Amazon has truly become a jungle. Authors and self publishers will do things on Amazon.com they would never consider doing offline. And it's often the "experts" who should know better who encourage them to do it!

What we need now is an etiquette for Amazon. I here propose several guidelines as a starting point.

1. *Don't flood.* Don't overwhelm Amazon with submissions for particular features. This includes creating loads of Listmania lists.

2. *Don't deceive.* Don't make something look like what it's not. This includes writing phony customer reviews, or soliciting reviews from people who can't sincerely and knowledgeably praise your book.

3. *Don't horn in.* Don't use the page for someone else's book to sell your own. This includes writing customer reviews mostly so you can recommend or mention your book. Exceptions are when Amazon reserves space for promoting other books, as with Best Value paid placements or Listmania lists.

4. *Don't attack.* Don't undercut a competitor's book in any way. This includes writing negative customer reviews. An exception is reporting to Amazon when you spot other authors or publishers ignoring these guidelines!

When in doubt, follow the Golden Rule. If you don't want it done to you—or if you don't want to see everyone else do the same—don't do it yourself!

---

* This is an update of an article I posted on my Publishing Page in 2007 in response to a now-popular book I found to be promoting spam techniques on Amazon. It's a matter close to my heart!

Kindle Books

I've advised you not to make your book available on Amazon in more than one format, because it can lead to lower collective sales ranking and therefore reduced overall sales. But sometimes—as for many self-published novels—sales and ranking are so low anyway, there's not much to lose. Offering a Kindle version may then be an attractive option, as you can offer it at a promotional price you couldn't match in print.

There's also the consideration that for some kinds of books—for example, extremely short works or light fiction—Kindle readers might in fact be your *best* market on Amazon. In that case, adding a Kindle version, or even choosing Kindle in place of POD, might make a lot of sense.

Though I'm no expert on publishing for the Kindle, here are a few tips that might prove useful if you go that route.

The Kindle format is basically a stripped-down version of HTML and CSS, the main languages used for Web pages. Because of the simplified code set, the formatting you can apply to your text is very limited. And because of hardware limitations, you can't yet do much with graphics either.

The easiest, most effective way to format a Kindle Book turns out to be—believe it or not—with Microsoft Word. Start with a Word document properly formatted for a book, then export to HTML. Yes, as you'll often be warned, this produces a huge, cluttered file, *but it doesn't matter.* Amazon will have no problem converting the code.

When you submit your book for the Kindle, Amazon's online form limits your title/subtitle combination to only 128 characters. So, you'll have to use your subtitle's short form here.

Amazon's submission form lets you specify an ISBN, but this is extremely misleading. Amazon does *not* list your ISBN with your Kindle Book, reveal it in search, or use it to identify the book in any way. Instead, it identifies the book by a completely arbitrary ASIN. So, if you list a unique ISBN for your Kindle Book on this form, you're throwing it away.

Then why does Amazon ask for it? Without mentioning this on the form, Amazon hopes you'll give the ISBN of a paperback or other *print* version of the book, to signify that the two should be linked. And you're supposed to guess that!

By report, submitting a print ISBN in this way does get your Kindle Book linked more quickly—but it should automatically be linked anyway in a week or two, assuming that at least the main titles are identical. Note that, since Amazon won't recognize an ISBN assigned to your Kindle Book itself—even if you submitted that ISBN on the form—you will *not* be able to request linking through the Books Content Update Form. That form will simply reject an ASIN that's not also an ISBN—so you'll be stuck.

For a Kindle Book, the sales rank shown on Amazon—and on Sales Rank Express—is its rank among Kindle Books only. So, it's not that hard for a Kindle Book to have an impressive sales rank!

To get info on Kindle publishing, to sign up, or to manage your account, go to Amazon's Digital Text Platform at

dtp.amazon.com

For Amazon's formatting instructions, visit its Digital Text Platform Community Support at

forums.digitaltextplatform.com/dtpforums

Publishing Reprints

Publishing has become so quick, cheap, and easy that many new small publishers are tempted to crank out books for volume. And where's the cheapest and most convenient place to find material? Old, out-of-copyright books. They're already written, edited, and in many cases, acceptably formatted. You don't have to hassle with an author or pay royalties, and even better, you don't have to come up with anything original.

The problem is that so many small publishers have had the same idea before you. So much so, that Amazon has become clogged with different editions of the same books. And in fact, Amazon has already put its foot down and said, "Enough!"

What happens is, if Amazon decides your book is too close in content to a number of others, it may simply choose to ignore it. Your book will not show up in search, so customers will not find it. It doesn't matter if your edition is somehow "better," or even if it was selling well for a time. Reportedly, it doesn't even matter if you publish it through BookSurge or CreateSpace. It can just disappear.

Even if it remains visible, you may find it stuck with descriptive content, customer reviews, and even Search Inside pages meant for other editions. So, even a superior edition may be branded by the errors and omissions of less conscientious publishers.

Amazon's message is clear: This particular path has been trod often enough. Give us something different!

Still, there are times when a small publisher may feel compelled to undertake a reprint as a labor of love. How can you keep your carefully cultivated edition from being thrown into the pot with all the rest?

I haven't trod this path myself—yet—but if and when I try a reprint, there are a couple of steps I will take. First, I'll alter the title. For instance, someday I hope to reprint a book called *Old Swedish Fairy Tales*, by Anna Wahlenberg. But I won't call it *Old Swedish Fairy Tales*. Instead, I'll call it *The Singing Tree, and Other Old Swedish Fairy Tales*. That will be more attractive, differentiate it from any other editions, and yet still come up in a search for the original title.

The most important thing, though, is that I will keep it out of Search Inside. If Amazon really is automating its search for similar content, then Search Inside has to be what it's using for it. Keep Amazon away from your content, and you stand a better chance of avoiding its interference.

Removing a Listing

It sometimes happens that a self publisher wants Amazon to remove a book entirely from its listings. Maybe that book or that edition was an early effort that's now more an embarrassment than an asset. Maybe it was a private project that was never even meant to be sold. How can you get Amazon to remove it?

Generally speaking, you can't. The Amazon catalog isn't a listing only of books for sale, much less only of ones you *want* to be for sale. It's a listing of books that might *ever* be for sale—by you, a Marketplace vendor, anyone. If the book exists and Amazon knows about it, it's there for good. And that's really not anyone else's business but Amazon's.

Of course, there are exceptions. One would be when the sale of a book would somehow expose Amazon to legal difficulty—for instance, if it was selling an edition that infringed on copyright. In that specific case, write directly to

copyright@amazon.com

Rogue Sellers

Amazon's Marketplace has become more and more dominated by commercial sellers wielding powerful software. This has made it vulnerable to attempts to scam the system.

For instance, there was the vendor who siphoned off info about all new Lightning Source books—apparently either from Lightning or from one of its distribution partners—and who then posted listings of these books on Amazon before the info could reach there through normal channels. While this could speed up the listing process by a day or more, it could also result in errors that the publisher had to watch for and correct. Luckily, this vendor is no longer with us.

Then there are the sellers, as described by Steve Weber, who list a book at two or three times its normal price and wait for unwary customers. This has evolved into an even more insidious practice: Posting a duplicate listing of the book under a new ASIN, making it look like that vendor is the book's only source.

If you find such a listing for one of your books, report it to Amazon immediately. Scroll to the bottom of that page and click on the link for submitting "other feedback." State that the listing is a duplicate, give the ASIN (ISBN-10) for the legitimate listing, insist that the duplicate listing be removed, and request that Amazon stop the deceptive practices of that vendor.

With luck, you might see the vendor vanish from Amazon entirely. At least under that name.

Amazon Vendors

Are you curious how the big publishers deal with Amazon? The answer is Amazon Vendors.

Basically, this program is like a big brother of Amazon Advantage. Just as Amazon has herded small publishers into Advantage, it has herded bigger publishers into Vendors—sometimes with threats to stop selling their books. Like Advantage, Vendors wants a 55% discount, though this and other terms may be negotiable. (Reportedly, publishers on the low end of the scale for this program have been able to reduce the discount to 40%, and even to get Amazon to pay shipping.)

Program members must accept returns, which are average for the book industry—in other words, high. And most contracts have required the publisher to pay back a significant percentage of sales in fees for dramatically overpriced marketing programs.

The benefits? Besides keeping Amazon from pulling the plug? Well, for one thing, these publishers are apt to get a lot more serious attention to their inquiries and complaints. But personally, I'd rather scrape along at the bottom of the tank and keep my short discount.

The online site for Amazon Vendors is Vendor Central—not to be confused with *Seller* Central, which is for Marketplace *vendors*. (Confused yet?) If you'd like to stand humbly before the gates to pay your respects, you can find it at

vendorcentral.amazon.com

Amazon Ref Codes

In my section on linking to Amazon, I discussed the parts of Amazon's Web page addresses actually needed for linking from outside, and I glossed over the parts for Amazon's internal use only. But while these other parts may not be immediately useful to the self publisher, they can provide intriguing glimpses into how Amazon operates. The most important of these parts is Amazon's referrer codes, or "ref codes," for short.

Every link from any Amazon page to any other includes a ref code to describe the location of that link. And that location includes not only the page that the link is on, but also the feature that displays the link, and the link's position relative to other links displayed by that feature.

Let's look again at a typical address you might collect from your browser's address bar while visiting one of Amazon's book detail pages. As before, this is like one you might see for *Aiming at Amazon.*

> http://www.amazon.com/Aiming-Amazon-
> Publishing-Marketing-Amazon-com/
> dp/093849743X/ref=sr_1_6?
> ie=UTF8&s=books&qid=1247001137&sr=1-6

Can you spot the ref code? Here it is on its own.

> ref=sr_1_6

What this code would tell you is that you reached this page by first performing a search ("sr") and then, on the first page of results, clicking on the sixth book listed. (Later in the address, a query ID—"qid"—tells Amazon exactly what search produced this positioning for this book, while the ref code is repeated in another format for programming convenience at the end.)

Here's another ref code, taken from a different link but to the same page.

ref=pd_sim_b_2

This one says that the link is from a feature based on purchase histories ("pd")—namely an Also Bought listing ("sim," short for "similar")—and that this linked item from the Books department ("b") was #2 on the list.

Amazon's ref codes, combined with sales history, help Amazon learn how best to design its pages and their features so you are directed to the books you want to see and then buy them. Every time you click on a link on Amazon, you are "voting" for that particular *kind* of link—and the more votes that kind gets, the more likely it is to keep its position or be moved somewhere more prominent.

On Amazon, everything is testing. Little is left to guesswork!

The Book Depository

If your book goes through Lightning Source directly or indirectly, you can recommend Amazon for almost all sales in North America and Europe. But what do you say to potential readers in Australia and New Zealand who can't buy from Amazon without paying a fortune in shipping?

The answer is to send them to The Book Depository, which handles all books printed by Lightning. This U.K.-based bookseller may charge a little more for the book, but shipping is free to many countries—and that includes Australia and New Zealand! Find it at

www.bookdepository.co.uk

or visit the U.S. store at

www.bookdepository.com

For a link, you can construct one in the following format, replacing the ISBN shown here for *Aiming at Amazon*.

http://www.bookdepository.co.uk/book/
9780938497431

For a keyword search, you can use a link like

http://www.bookdepository.co.uk/search?
searchTerm=Aiming+Amazon+Shepard

To become an affiliate and earn commissions, go to

affiliates.bookdepository.co.uk

Replica Books

Though I discussed the two major POD publisher services in the U.S. today—BookSurge Publisher Services and Lightning Source—there's a third you might want to know about. Replica Books, a division of the second largest U.S. wholesaler, Baker & Taylor, is almost as old as Lightning Source, and started out with great promise. But through increasing neglect and lack of integration with the wholesale operation, Replica dwindled to the point of barely functioning.

Now, though, seeing the growing success and importance of Lightning Source, B&T has got religion. Plans are to open a new POD center at a B&T distribution facility in September 2009, operated for the wholesaler by the international printing company R. R. Donnelly. For the first time, all books from Replica will be listed and shown as always available in the B&T catalog, and a Web site will finally be developed for publisher clients.

In the past, Replica has allowed its publishers to set their own discounts and returns policy, just like Lightning Source. Whether this continues to be true, and whether the new Replica will be any more welcoming of small publishers than the old one was, remains to be seen. But if so, Replica may offer Lightning publishers a prime opportunity for double-sourcing—making books available from more than one printer/distributor for safety of supply—and for complementing Lightning's strengths with alternate ones.

To note progress, keep your eye on

www.replicabooks.com

Self Publishing Terms

In my books, I refer to POD author services with the common term "self publishing company." Many Old Guard self publishers object to this term, saying customers of these companies are not really self publishing at all, and insisting the companies be called vanity publishers or subsidy publishers instead.

But this is just playing Humpty Dumpty with the language. A self publisher is anyone who pays the money and makes the decisions—and any company enabling that process has every right to call itself a "self publishing company."

Vanity publishing is itself a subset of self publishing, and always has been. *Subsidy publishing*, on the other hand, means that the author *shares* in the publisher's costs and control. Since these modern companies invest nothing at all of their own in their books' success, they are definitely *not* subsidy publishers!

Author Online!

For updates and more resources,
visit Aaron Shepard's Publishing Page at

www. newselfpublishing.com

Index

Aaron Shepard's Publishing
  Blog, 11
Aaron Shepard's Publishing
  Page, 11, 25, 119, 172, 202–
  203
accounts (Amazon), 64, 172, 185
Adobe Acrobat, 51, 56
Adobe Illustrator, 51, 192
Adobe InDesign, 48–49, 56
Adobe Photoshop and
  Photoshop Elements, 50, 56
Aiming at Amazon, 13, 15, 60,
  76–77, 83, 95, 107, 109, 112,
  118, 159, 166–167, 175, 180,
  191, 193, 200, 211, 213
Also Bought listings (Amazon),
  36, 42, 128, 143–145, 148,
  151, 157, 179, 198, 212
Amapedia, 125
Amazon, 10–11, 14–24, 26–28,
  30–45, 48, 53–60, 63–129,
  131–149, 151–159, 161–182,
  184–196, 198–200, 203–213
Amazon Advantage, 27, 30, 68,
  75, 86, 92, 96–97, 164, 210
Amazon Associates, 164, 168,
  172
Amazon Blog, 118–119
Amazon Friends, 70, 115, 122
Amazon Joyo (China), 184
Amazon Marketplace, 30, 75,
  82, 101, 190, 208–210
Amazon POD, 18–22, 28, 76,
  132–133, 139, 182

Amazon Profile, 67, 70, 99, 106,
  108, 114, 116, 122–123, 125,
  155
Amazon Shorts, 94
Amazon Upgrade, 126
Amazon Vendors, 210
Amazon Vine, 114
Amazon Web Services, 164
Amazon.ca (Canada), 64, 182,
  184–187, 189, 191, 193–194,
  199
Amazon.co.jp (Japan), 182,
  184–187, 189, 191, 193–195,
  199–200
Amazon.co.uk (U.K.), 18, 64,
  182, 184–187, 189–191, 193–
  194, 198–200
Amazon.com (U.S.), 14–15, 18–
  19, 22, 27, 35, 64–71, 77, 79,
  83, 87, 95–96, 99–101, 106–
  108, 110, 112, 114, 116, 120,
  123, 125–127, 135, 140, 153,
  159, 164–172, 182, 184, 186,
  189, 191–192, 194, 196, 198–
  200, 203, 208, 210–211
Amazon.de (Germany), 18, 64,
  182, 184–187, 189, 191, 193–
  195, 199–200
Amazon.fr (France), 64, 182,
  184–187, 189, 191, 193, 196,
  199–200
AmazonConnect, 80, 117
anthologies, 105
Apple, 32

ASIN (Amazon Standard Identification Number), 68, 76–78, 81, 83, 112, 133, 153, 167, 169, 191, 193, 205, 209
Australia, 19, 183, 213
Author Central (Amazon), 67, 79–80, 82–85, 110, 116–117, 120
Author Pages, 79–81, 116–117, 119–120, 123, 125, 189
AuthorHouse, 17, 21
availability listings (Amazon), 75–76, 132, 141, 154, 189–190, 192
Baker & Taylor, 19, 43, 214
banks and bank accounts, 164, 199
bar codes, 24, 55, 76
Barnes & Noble, 19, 26
BarnesandNoble.com (BN.com), 162
Bertrams|THE, 189
Best Value placements (Amazon), 127, 144, 203
bestsellers, 14, 35, 37, 109–110, 129–130, 136, 140
Bestsellers (Amazon feature), 110
Better Together placements (Amazon), 144
bindings and binding, 34, 83, 191
blogs, bloggers, and blogging, 117
Book Catalog Department (Amazon), 68–69, 85, 92, 110, 133, 179
Book Depository, The, 75, 213
Booklocker, 17, 21
Books & Writers Rank Monitoring Service, 136

Books Content Update Form (Amazon), 87, 89–90, 102, 110, 179, 205
Books, Typography, and Microsoft Word, 59
bookstores, 14–16, 19, 22, 26–28, 34, 37, 53–54, 162
BookSurge, 17–22, 24, 27–28, 76, 132–133, 135, 139, 182, 206, 214
BookSurge Publisher Services, 18, 24, 27, 214
Borders and Borders.com, 19
Bowker, R. R., and BowkerLink, 14, 29
Business of Writing for Children, The, 15, 33, 40, 42, 58, 84, 134, 137, 174
BXGY (Buy X, Get Y) marketing program (Amazon), 126, 128
Canada, 18, 183–187, 190–191, 193–196, 199
catalog rebuilds (Amazon), 142–143
Catalog Update Form (Amazon), 82–83, 87, 90, 154, 178, 192, 194
categories, book (Amazon), 109–110, 126, 140–141, 144
chaining (Sales Rank Express), 146
Chicago Manual of Style, The, 48
children's books, 34
China, 184, 197
CMYK (color mode), 56
Community Help (Amazon), 69, 153
Complete Idiot's Guide to Self-Publishing, The, 49
consultants, publishing, 25, 129, 202

contact forms (Amazon), 67–69, 85, 92, 110, 133, 153, 179, 186–187

copyright, 46, 48, 208

copyright page, 48

corrections, data, 81–85, 87, 90, 154, 174, 180, 193

cover and cover image, book, 37, 42, 53–55, 74, 82, 85, 93–94, 96–98, 101–103, 117–118, 122, 124, 175, 196

cover price, 15, 21, 26–27, 33, 75, 147

CreateSpace, 17–23, 28, 33–34, 76, 132–133, 135, 139, 182, 206

credit cards, 65, 111

currencies, 10, 17, 121, 127, 129, 156, 164, 178, 189–190, 199

Customer Discussions (Amazon), 125

Customer Images (Amazon), 65, 98–99, 102

Customer Reviews (Amazon), 37, 45, 48, 58 59, 67, 70, 88, 111–115, 122, 153–156, 176, 179, 198, 203, 206

Customer Reviews Discussion Board (Amazon), 114

desktop publishing, 9, 25, 47

detail pages, book (Amazon), 98–99, 106, 108, 112, 117, 123, 125, 148, 193, 211

Digital Text Platform (Amazon), 205

Digital Text Platform Community Support (Amazon), 205

discounts, 26–28, 30, 75–76, 126–127, 144, 190, 210, 214

distribution, book, 17–22, 24, 190, 209, 214

distributors, book, 26, 214

draw programs, 51

drop shipping, 19, 132–133, 137–138, 189

ebooks, 57, 59, 94, 113

Editorial Reviews (Amazon), 87, 89–92, 125

editors and editing, 46, 50, 58, 60, 84, 108, 116, 118–119

Elements of Style, The, 45

ethics, professional, 108, 111–113, 115, 153–154, 156, 177, 203, 209

exit offers (Amazon), 145

Features and Services contact form (Amazon), 67, 69, 153, 186

fiction, 10, 32, 38, 41, 46, 48, 100, 105, 115, 204

Fine Print of Self Publishing, The, 21

Fix Data button (Sales Rank Express), 83, 193

fonts and typefaces, 48–49, 51

France, 184–187, 191, 193–197, 199

Frequently Bought Together placements (Amazon), 127, 144–146, 152, 198

FTP (File Transfer Protocol), 96, 101

Gardners Books, 189

General Questions contact form (Amazon), 67–68, 85, 92, 110, 133, 179, 186

Germany, 64, 182, 184–187, 191, 193–195, 197, 199

Get Pairings button (Sales Rank Express), 42, 136, 138, 146–147

Get Versions button (Sales Rank Express), 88

Google, 39, 41–42, 159, 168, 188, 196
Google Insights for Search, 41
Google Translate, 188, 196
graphics, 33–34, 45, 48, 50–51, 53–56, 58, 93, 95, 98, 100, 116–120, 162, 192, 204
hardcovers, 35, 57, 88–89
HTML (Hypertext Markup Language), 90, 116, 118–120, 164, 172, 204
indexes and indexing, 170–172, 200, 217
Infinity Publishing, 17, 21
Ingram Book Company, 19, 26, 28, 43, 74–75, 84, 132–133, 137–139, 189
invoicing, 20
ipage (Ingram), 84
ISBN (International Standard Book Number), 24, 29, 55, 68, 74, 76–78, 81, 87–88, 95, 135, 167, 170, 176–179, 190–191, 205, 213
iUniverse, 17, 21
Japan, 182, 184–187, 191, 193–197, 199
Jobs, Steve, 32
keywords, 39–44, 105–106, 168, 170, 213
Kindle and Kindle Books, 57, 204–205
Kremer, John, 9
languages and translation, 10, 46, 48, 107, 171, 184–193, 195–198, 200, 204, 215
libraries and library market, 19–20, 77, 109, 192
Library of Congress, 77
Lightning Source, 18–19, 21, 24–28, 33, 43, 55, 74–75, 87, 132–133, 135, 138–139, 163,

182, 189–190, 196, 202, 209, 213–214
Lightning Source UK, 189, 196
linked formats and editions (Amazon), 88, 143, 148, 178–179, 199, 205, 211
linking, book (Amazon), 88, 178–179, 199, 205, 211
Listmania lists (Amazon), 122–124, 141, 159, 203
litho printing (offset), 18, 102
Lulu.com, 17, 22
Microsoft Access, 184, 187
Microsoft Visio, 51
Microsoft Windows, 51, 84, 136
Microsoft Word, 48–49, 51–52, 55, 204
MySpace, 122, 125
New Zealand, 213
news releases (Amazon), 71
Nielsen BookData, 189, 196
nonfiction, 10, 32–33, 35, 38, 41, 46, 100, 105, 109, 115, 174, 176
Notepad (Windows), 84
novels, 38, 41, 48, 105, 204
offset printing (litho), 18, 102
Outskirts Press, 17, 21
page layout programs, 48, 51
paid placements (Amazon), 126–127, 144, 146, 203
pairings (Amazon), 36, 42, 104, 128, 136, 143–148, 151–152, 157, 179, 198, 212
paperbacks, 33, 35, 57, 88, 205
PDF (Portable Document Format) and PDF files, 51, 56, 58, 100–101, 180
PDF/A, 51
Perfect Pages, 52, 55, 59
photo-paint programs, 50
POD for Profit, 28

pod_publishers (Yahoo group), 202

Poynter, Dan, 9, 37, 125

prices and pricing, 26, 28, 33, 55, 57, 75, 154, 163, 190, 204, 209

print on demand (POD), 9–11, 17–21, 24, 26, 30, 32–33, 50–51, 174, 176–177

printers, inkjet, 17, 34

printers, laser, 9, 17

printing, book, 17–19, 21–22, 26, 28, 33–34, 51, 55–56, 101, 133, 146, 189, 214

printing, color, 34

Print-on-Demand (Yahoo group), 202

Product Advertising API, 164–165

ProductWikis, 125

proofreaders and proofreading, 50, 58

publication date, 178

Publishers and Book Sellers Guide (Amazon), 66

Publishers Weekly, 127

publishing names, 24

R. R. Donnelly, 214

Rankforest, 136

RankTracer, 136

Real Names (Amazon), 111

referrer codes, Amazon, 211–212

Relevance search order (Amazon), 44, 141, 175, 191

Replica Books, 214

reprints and reprinting, 174, 206–207

returns, 16, 210, 214

reviews, 45, 58, 60–61, 65, 78, 89–92, 111–115, 118, 125–126, 138, 153–156, 159, 203

rivalries and rivals (Amazon), 148–150, 152

Rosenthal, Morris, 36, 110, 137

Ross, Tom and Marilyn, 9

royalties, 15, 21, 26, 206

RSS (Really Simple Syndication), 120

S.R.E. Web Widget (Sales Rank Express), 136, 164

Sales Rank Express (S.R.E.), 36, 42, 72, 76–77, 83, 86–88, 132–133, 135–136, 138, 146–147, 152–153, 157, 165, 185–186, 190, 193–194, 198, 205

sales ranks (Amazon), 35–37, 72, 75, 109, 114, 121, 135–138, 140–141, 144, 148, 198, 204–205

SalesRankWatcher, 136

scans and scanning, 51

schools and school market, 19–20

screening and descreening, 119

search and search results, 39–40, 42, 44, 53, 57, 74, 88, 96, 100–102, 104, 116, 132, 136, 141–143, 151, 157–158, 162, 168, 179, 197

search engines and SEO (search engine optimization), 39, 42, 168

Search Inside (Amazon), 44, 53, 94, 100–103, 126, 141, 144, 206–207

Search Suggestions (Amazon), 106

self publishing companies, 9, 17–26, 28, 45, 87–88, 133, 135, 139, 182, 202, 215

Self-Publishing Manual, The, 37, 125

Sell on Amazon, 30

Seller Central (Amazon), 30, 101, 210
Shepard Publications, 64
short discount, 26–27, 76, 163, 210
Small Vendor Co-op Merchandising (SVC) marketing program (Amazon), 126–128
Smart Soapmaking, 148–152, 157–158, 183
SNP (Single New Product) marketing program (Amazon), 128
So You'd Like to . . . guides, 124–125, 159
Southeast Asia, 19
spine, book cover, 55
spin-offs, 51, 123–125, 197, 203
Stine, R. L., 39
stock and stocking, 15, 19–20, 27, 75, 132–134, 138–139, 180, 189, 192
subsidy publishers and publishing, 215
table of contents, 90–91
tags and tagging (Amazon), 65, 78, 104–108, 118–119, 141, 144, 157–159, 168, 170–171, 196–197
Tags for Amazon Search, 106–108
testimonials, 58–61, 89, 91–92, 115, 118, 120
TextEdit (Mac), 84
title page, 48
titles and subtitles, 14, 17–19, 36, 39–44, 48, 53–55, 68, 74, 78, 82–83, 85, 93, 105–106, 116–117, 122, 135–136, 141, 144, 146–147, 153, 168, 170,

174–175, 178–180, 192, 197, 204–205, 207
TitleZ, 136
Top Reviewers (Amazon), 113–115
Top Self Publishing Companies, 21
Trafford, 17, 21
Ultimately Buy listings (Amazon), 148–152, 198
United Kingdom (U.K.), 19, 24, 28, 182–187, 189–191, 193–194, 196, 199–200, 213
United States (U.S.), 10, 14, 18–19, 22, 24, 28–29, 64–65, 164, 182–184, 188–190, 199–200, 213–214
updating in place, 177–178, 180
vanity publishers and publishing, 215
Vendor Central (Amazon), 210
videos and video production, 90, 118–119
Watson, Anne L., 38, 41, 60, 148, 150, 152, 157–158, 174, 183
Web sites, building and running, 47, 119, 136, 162, 164, 172, 199
Weber, Steve, 30, 209
wholesalers, book, 19, 22, 26, 28, 30, 82, 132, 189–190, 214
Wikipedia, 125, 197
word processors, 48–49, 51, 84, 116, 118, 176
Wordclay, 17, 21
WordTracker, 41
XHTML (Extensible Hypertext Markup Language), 118
Xlibris, 17, 21
Yahoo Groups, 133, 183, 202
YouTube, 119

About the Author

Aaron Shepard is a foremost proponent of the *new* business of profitable self publishing through print on demand, which he has practiced and helped develop since 1999. Unlike most authorities on self publishing, he makes the bulk of his living from his self-published books—not from consulting, speaking, freelance writing, or selling publishing services. In an alternate life, Aaron is an award-winning children's author with numerous picture books from publishers both large and small. He lives in Friday Harbor, Washington, in the San Juan Islands, with his wife and fellow author, Anne L. Watson.

How This Book Was Made

This book was made on a Mac. The pages were created in Microsoft Word, and the cover in Adobe InDesign. PDF files were produced and processed with Adobe Acrobat Pro. The interior text font is 12-point Georgia with 15-point linespacing, and the cover typeface is Verdana.

Version History

1.0   September 8, 2006
1.1   September 17, 2006
1.2   September 24, 2006
1.2.1   December 26, 2007
1.2.2   May 3, 2008
2.0   December 26, 2008
2.1   August 5, 2009

Breinigsville, PA USA
07 March 2011
257132BV00003B/58/P